Summer Fit Activities™

First to Second Grade

Build Fit Brains and Fit Bodies!

 Fun, skill based activities in reading, writing, mathematics, and language arts with additional activities in science and geography. Curriculum activities are based on national standards.

 Summer Fitness program includes aerobic and strength exercises.. Fitness log, exercise videos and instructions included. Keeping young bodies active and strong helps children live better, learn more and feel healthier.

 Incentive Contract Calendars motivate children to complete activities and exercises by rewarding their efforts. Summer Explorers are lists of fun and active things to do — perfect for when your child says, "I'm bored, what can I do?"

 Core values and role model activities include child activities, parent talking points and reading lists.

 Summer Journaling, Book Reports, Health and Nutrition Index, Certificate of Completion and Flashcards.

Access more summer resource materials at
www.SummerFitActivities.com

Written by: Kelly Terrill and Portia Marin

Fitness and Nutrition: Lisa Roberts RN, BSN, PHN, Coach James Cordova and Charles Miller

Cover Illustration: Amanda Sorensen

Illustrations: Roxanne Ottley, Amanda Sorensen, Fernando Becerra,
  Richard Casillas, Jason Gould, Bess Li, Sarah Shah

Page Layout: Robyn Pettit

Special Thanks: Wildlife SOS

For orders or product information call 801-466-4272

Dedication

Summer Fit™ is dedicated to Julia Hobbs and Carla Fisher who are the original authors of Summer Bridge Activities™. Julia and Carla helped pioneer summer learning and dedicated their lives to their vocation of teaching.

Caution

Exercises may require adult supervision. If you have any concerns regarding your child's ability to complete any of the suggested fitness activities, consult your family doctor or pediatrician. Children should always stretch and warm up before exercises. Do not push children past comfort level or ability. Exercises were created to be fun for parents and caregivers as well as the child, but not as a professional training or weight loss program. Exercise should stop immediately if you or your child experiences any of the following symptoms: pain, feeling dizzy or faint, nausea, or severe fatigue.

Copyright

Printed in the USA   All Rights Reserved   ISBN 978-0-9982902-2-5

Table of Contents

★ = Academic   ● = Core Value   ▲ = Fitness   ■ =Writing   = Play & Do   ◆ = Track

Dear Parent,

As a mother, I value giving my children the academic resources they need for success in both their personal and school life. However, when summer comes it is hard to resist the urge to shutter the books and toss the backpacks in the closet.

I have learned first hand that the lack of study over the summer holiday can cause summer learning loss. Studies show that as much as 2.5 months of learning can be undone and some children have lower test scores during the period directly after summer. It is important to find a balance between summer vacation and homework. **Summer Fit Activities** is the resource that does it while looking and feeling like academic summer camp.

Summer Fit Activities is an engaging workbook that helps your child learn and grow. It contains three different foundation pieces for your child's success: academics, health, and values that help children become kinder, more empathetic and stronger leaders. **Summer Fit Activities** makes learning fun with colorful illustrations, family activities, fitness logs, and incentive calendars. Summer Fit is easy to use for parents, caregivers and even grandparents, because day-by-day lesson plans are straightforward and flexible to allow you to create a summer learning experience specifically for your child.

Summer Fit Activities educates the whole child just like you would in summer camp- with an emphasis on FUN. My children love the healthy snack ideas they can make on their own and the Summer Explorer lists of outdoor learning activities that provide hands on learning experiences. I love the flashcards included in the back of book to help reinforce basic skills and the peace of mind knowing that I am teaching my child to be a great person, as well as a great student.

Summer is a time for adventure and fun, but it is also a time of learning and growth. With **Summer Fit Activities** I found the balance I was looking for - unplug, learn and let the magic of summer unfold before your eyes!

Have a wonderful summer,

Christa
Parent

INSIDE
Summer Fit Activities™

Here is what you will find inside Summer Fit™:

Academics

- There are 5 sections of academic exercises, each section with its own core value and journal entry page.

- Sections begin with Incentive Contract Calendars and "Summer Fitness Logs."

- Your child will complete activities in reading, writing, math and language arts. Science and geography activities are included throughout the book.

- When your child completes each day, he/she may color or initial the academic and reading icon for that day on the Incentive Contract Calendar.

- Parents initial the Incentive Contract Calendar once the section has been completed.

Fitness

Research shows that keeping bodies strong and healthy helps children learn better, live better and even miss fewer days of school! To keep bodies healthy, children need to eat right, get enough sleep and exercise daily.

- The Summer Fitness Program helps children set goals and track performance over the summer.

- Daily aerobic and strength exercises

- Fitness & Health Index includes Nutrition page, Foods to Eat Everyday & Meal Tracker.

- Online videos show the proper way to complete exercises.

Values Education

Core values are fundamental to society and are incorporated into our civil laws. Research shows that character education is more effective when parents encourage values in their child's daily routine. Core values are vitally important to the overall growth, well-being and success of all children.

- Each section highlights two different values and role models.

- Value activities are designed for children and parents.

- Each value includes a reading comprehension activity based on role models from throughout the world.

Helpful Hints for Summer Fit™

 Flip through the book to become familiar with the layout and activities. Look ahead to the upcoming core value so you can incorporate discussions and activities into your daily routine.

 Provide your child with the tools he/she will need to complete the work: pencils, pens, crayons, ruler, and healthy dose of encouragement.

 Try to set aside a specific time to do Summer Fit™ each day (for example, after breakfast each morning). Make sure your child has enough time to complete the day's work and exercise.

 Be a cheerleader! Encourage your child to do their best, urging them to challenge themselves. Make sure they know you are there to help them if they need support. Talk about and reinforce the material in the book beyond the page. For example, after reading about insects, encourage your child to find an insect in the yard to observe and draw.

 Look at your child's work frequently. Make sure they know you value what they are doing and it is not just "busywork".

 Try doing Summer Fit™ outside in the fresh air: at the park, in the backyard, camping, or on the beach. Summer Fit™ can go wherever you go!

 Ask older siblings, grandparents, babysitters and even friends to participate in and give one on one help with the activities. Summer Fit™ is great shared experience!

 Keep up with the Incentive Contract Calendars. Follow through and reward completed work: stamps, stickers, hugs, and high fives are great ways to motivate and recognize a job well done.

 Let your child do more than one page at a sitting if he/she is enthusiastic and wants to work ahead. Make sure to check the website for additional activities and resources that can help you tailor Summer Fit™ to your child's needs.

 When the book has been completed, display the Certificate of Completion proudly and let your child know what a great job he/she did. Celebrate!

Encourage Summer Reading and Writing

> Reading and writing skills are important skills for your child's success. Summer is a great time to encourage and build reading and writing skills with your child regardless of ability.
>
> You can do many things to encourage literacy and writing:

 Make Reading a Priority: Create a routine by establishing a reading time each day for your child.

 Read Around Your Child: Read in front of him/her as much as possible. Talk with your child about the books you are reading.

 Create a Summer Reading List: Find books that involve your child's favorite interests like sports, art, mysteries, dance, etc.

 Reading On The Road: Billboards, menus, street signs, window banners and packaging labels are great ways to reinforce reading comprehension skills.

 Storytelling: Have campfire nights in your backyard and tell stories about things you did when you were their age. Slip in a few scary spooks as well!

 Read Together: Newspapers, magazine articles and stories on the Internet are great to read together and discuss.

 Library Time: Go to the library on a weekly basis to choose new books.

 Letter Writing: Encourage your child to write thank you notes and letters.

 Plan a Trip: Have your child plan a trip for the family. Have him/her write an overview of the trip including where, what to bring, how to travel, how long and what you will do on your trip.

 Create a Joke Book: Provide a list of subjects for your child to create jokes about.

 Family Writing Hour: Sit down as a family and write a story together. Read the story out loud at the end.

 Script Writing: Ask your child to write a movie script. When it is finished, perform it as a family – be sure to video the production!

 Poetry: Discuss different forms of poetry. Have your child write a poem. Add an illustration.

Mindfulness

As a parent or guardian it is easy to get pulled into the many distractions of daily life. Have you ever wondered if your child has the same difficulties juggling personal interests with school with all the beeps, phone calls and text messages along the way?

Multitasking, compounded with technology, can make it difficult for all of us to concentrate on what we are doing in the moment. Growing research shows that we are hard wired to focus on one thing at a time. Teaching your child to be mindful and to focus on their internal feelings allows your child to fully experience what they are doing in the moment and can have a lasting effect on what, how and why they learn. Learning to sit without distractions and to focus on the moment is a gradual process that has immense benefits for you and your child.

Parent Tips to Help Children Be Mindful

 Time Set a time when all noises, distractions and devices are turned off — start with 5 minutes a day.

 Talk Ask your child to clear her thoughts and to focus on not thinking about anything.

 Focus Focus on breathing, take deep breathes and exhale slowly.

 Quiet Sit in silence.

 Show Show your child gratitude by thanking her for her time. Ask her what she is thankful for and discuss the importance of being grateful.

1-2 • © Summer Fit Activities™

Living Earth Friendly

We all share this home called Earth, and each one of us needs to be responsible in helping take care of her. There are many things families can do together to REDUCE, REUSE, and RECYCLE in order to be kind to Mother Earth. We can all BE SMART AND DO OUR PART!

There are many opportunities each day for us to practice these little steps with our children and we should talk with them about how little things add up to make a big impact.

REDUCE, REUSE, RECYCLE

REDUCE: Means to use less of something. Encourage your children to use water wisely, turn off lights when leaving a room, and use your own bags at the grocery store.

REUSE: Means to use an item again. Refill water bottles, wash dishes and containers instead of using disposable, mend or repair the things you have before buying new, and donate clothes and toys to be used by someone else.

RECYCLE: Means to make a new thing out of an old one. Recycle cans, bottles, and newspapers. Participate in local environmental initiatives like recycling drives.

REBUY: Means to purchase items that have already been used or recycled. Shop at thrift and consignment stores and when possible buy items that have been made from recycled materials.

1-2 • © Summer Fit Activities™

Summer Fitness Program

Choose a strength or cardio exercise for each day of academic activities. Check the box ✓ each day you complete your fitness activity. Fill in the Fitness Log on the back of each Incentive Contract Calendar. Choose exercises from the Health and Nutrition section in the back of the book. Exercise videos can be viewed at **www.SummerFitActivities.com**.

	Date	Stretch	Activity	Time
1.	*examples:* June 4	Run in place	Sky Reach	7 min
2.	June 5	Toe Touches	Bottle Curls	15 min
3.				
4.				
5.				

Let's Move!

Warm Up! Get ready to exercise by stretching and moving around.

Stretch! Move your head slowly side to side, try to touch each shoulder. Now move your head forward, touch your chin to your chest, then look up and as far back as you can. Try to touch your back with the back of your head.

Touch your toes when standing. Bend over at the waist and touch the end of your toes or the floor. Hold this position for 10 seconds.

Move! Walk or jog in place for 3-5 minutes to warm up before you exercise. Shake your arms and roll your shoulders when you are finished.

Summer Skill Review - Grade 1   MATH

Find out where your child needs a little extra practice!

1. Add or Subtract.

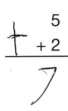

| 5
+ 2 | 1
+ 9 | 2
+ 6 | 6
- 4 | 8
- 3 | 9
- 5 |

7   10   8   2

---

2. What time is it?

_____ : _____   _____ : _____

3. Look at the + fact : 5 + 8 = 13

Write a second + fact: ____ + ___ = ___

Look at the – fact: 13 – 8 = 5

Write a second – fact: ____ - ___ = ___

---

4. Fill in the missing numbers.

5 __6__ 7 __8__ 9 __10__ 11 __12__

18 __9__ 20 __21__ 22 __23__ 24 __25__

35 __36__ 37 __38__ 39 __40__ 41 __42__

5. Fill in the sign. >,<,=

9 __<__ 10

3 + 4 __>__ 2 + 2

0 + 6 __=__ 6 + 0

---

6. What is the number?

4 tens 3 ones = _____

6 tens 2 ones = _____

2 tens 7 ones = _____

7. How many?

★ ★ ★ ★ ★ ★ ★

★ ★ ★ ★   _____

Circle the 5th star

Summer Skill Review - Grade 1   MATH

Find out where your child needs a little extra practice!

---

8. Draw a square. | **Draw a triangle.**

---

9. What is the value of the coins?

Quarter = 25 ¢

Dime = 10 ¢

Nickle = 5 ¢

Penny = 1 ¢

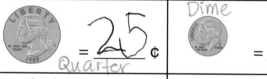
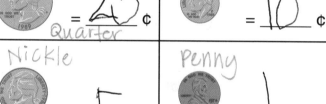

10. Dogs ‖‖‖ ‖

Cats ‖‖‖

How many dogs? 7 cats? 5

---

11. What month is missing?

January, February, ___March___, April

12. There were 9 birds in the tree.

3 flew away, how many birds left?

___6___

---

13. Color ¼ of the circle.

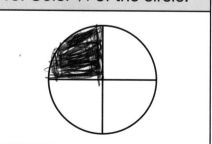

14. Finish counting by 2's.

2, _4_, 6, _8_, 10, _12_, 14, _16_, 18, _20_

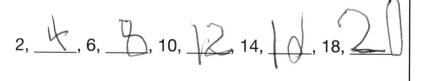

---

15. Write the numeral.
Nine ___9___
Fifteen ___15___

16. Finish counting by 10's.

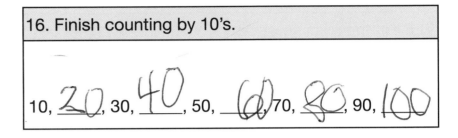

10, _20_, 30, _40_, 50, _60_, 70, _80_, 90, _100_

Grade 1-2 Language Arts Assessment

1. Circle what rhymes with cat.
(sat) (bat) rake (mat)
Circle what rhymes with ten?
pin (men) (hen) (den)

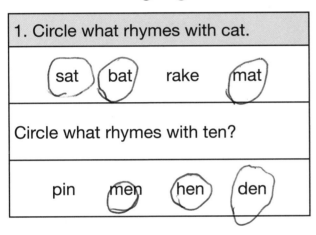

2. Write a noun to go with each.

adjective.

soft _Sock_   tall _window_

furry _ban_   hot _Sun_

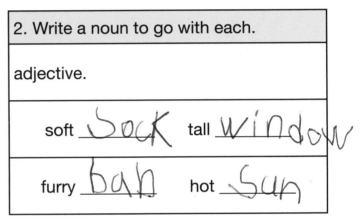

3. Circle the nouns in the sentence.
The (boy) rode his (bike) to the (park).

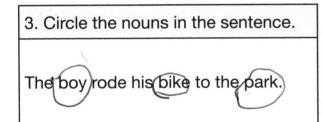

4. Underline the pronouns.

Sam and (I) went swimming. (We) swam in (his) pool all day.

5. Circle the letters that should have a capital.

(M)y Grandma (m)ary lives in (u)tah on (m)aple (s)treet.

6. Write the sentence in the correct order.

tire flat has a bike my ___My bike has a flat tire.___

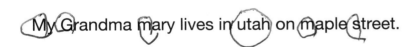

7. Fill in the missing verbs.

I like to ___ride___ my bike.	I will ___simm___ in the pool all day.

8. Read the following sight words. Circle any you don't know.

when	take	some	were	after
again	know	then	could	of

9. Write your first and last name: ___Emma Goddard___

10. Copy this sentence in your best handwriting: The butterfly landed on the red rose.

_____

_____

11. Fill in a vowel to make a word (a, e, i, o, u).

c_a_t   p_e_n   t_a_p   d_o_g   r_u_n   c_a_n   m_a_n

12. Write the contraction for each set of words.

I am = ___I'm___   it is = ___it's___   we will = ___we'll___

INCENTIVE CONTRACT CALENDAR

My parents and I agree that if I complete this section of

Summer Fit Activities™

and read ___20___ minutes a day, my reward will be _____

Child Signature: _____   Parent Signature: _____

Day 1			Day 6		
Day 2			Day 7		
Day 3			Day 8		
Day 4			Day 9		
Day 5			Day 10		

Color the for each day of activities completed.

Color the for each day of reading completed.

Summer Fitness Log

Choose your exercise activity each day from the Aerobic and Strength Activities in the back of the book. Record the date, stretch, activity and how long you performed your exercise activity below. Fill in how many days you complete your fitness activity on your Incentive Contract Calendars.

	Date	Stretch	Activity	Time
examples:	June 4	Run in place	Sky Reach	7 min
	June 5	Toe Touches	Bottle Curls	15 min
1.				
2.				
3.				
4.				
5.				
6.				
7.				
8.				
9.				
10.				

I promise to do my best for me. I exercise to be healthy and active. I am awesome because I am me.

Child Signature: _____

Missing letters

Write the letters to finish naming each picture.

b __ug	h __at__	t __op__	b __ee__
s __un__	d __og__	p __ig__	t __en__
t __ree__	g __oat__	c __at__	b __oat__
s __tar__	m __op__	f __eet__	c __ar__

Write the missing word from each rhyming pair.

1.	Ex. cat	2.	tree
3.	star	4.	boat

Numbers and Math - Mixed Practice

Add or subtract.

1. 4 – 2 = __2__

2. 3 + 5 = __8__

3. 2 - 1 = __1__

4. 6 - 3 = __3__

5. 3 + 3 = __6__

6. 5 - 2 = __3__

7. 4 + 4 = __8__

8. 2 + 8 = __10__

Circle the right amount of coins.

| 9. 50 cents = |  25 5 10 10 |
| 10. 25 cents = | |

Count by 2s to finish the pattern.

11. 2, __4__, 6, __8__, 10, __12__, 14, __16__, 18, __20__, 22

Choose your STRENGTH exercise!

Exercise for today:
ballet

Day 1

Check & Record in Fitness Log.

1-2 • © Summer Fit Activities™

SummerFitActivities.com

Healthy Choices

I can choose to be healthy. Circle the healthy choices.

Math - Measurement

How many inches long?

1. Worm is_____ inches.

2. Fly is _____ inch.

3. Grasshopper is _____ inches.

4. Comb is _____ inches.

5. Feather is _____ inches.

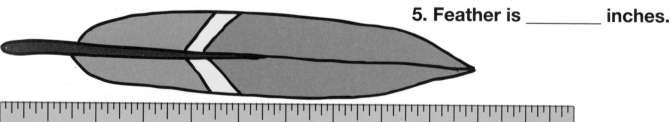

Choose your **AEROBIC** exercise!

Exercise for today:

Check & Record in Fitness Log.

Day 2

Beginning Sounds – Find the Beginning Sound

Long vowel sounds say their name a, e, i, o, u.

short

long

On each line say the word, write **L** if you hear a long vowel sound and **S** if you hear a short vowel sound.

1.	(kite)	L	8.	(bed) S
2.	(cat)	S	9.	(pin) S
3.	(umbrella)	S	10.	(gorilla) L
4.	(feet)	L	11.	(fox) S
5.	(boat)	L	12.	(shell) S
6	(top)	S	13.	(box) b
7.	10	S	14.	(cheese) b

Look at the time. Circle the correct answer.

1. School starts at 8:00. Sam is...

early   late   on time

2. Lunch is at 12:00. Sam is...

early   late   on time

3. Bedtime is 9:00. Sam is...

early   late   on time

Write the time.

4. _____   5. _____   6. _____

Count by 5s

5,___,15,___,25,___,35,___,45,___,55,___,65,___,75,___,85,___,95,___

Choose your STRENGTH exercise!

Exercise for today:

Check & Record in Fitness Log.

Day 3

Parts of a Plant

Label the parts of the flower and color.

Word key: parts of a plant				
blossom	leaf	stem	roots	seedling

1. blossom

2. leaf

3. seedling

4. stem

5. roots

Hands On

Fill a plastic cup with potting soil and plant some flower seeds or presoaked beans. Put in a sunny window, keep moist, and observe the growth of your plant.

6   is more than   4   2   is less than   5

Draw hungry alligators eating more. They always eat the bigger number.

3  9   7  5

11  10   0  1

15  20   10  3

Finish the pattern.

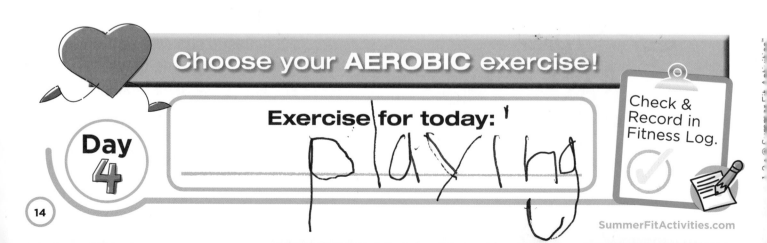

Choose your AEROBIC exercise!

Exercise for today: playing

Check & Record in Fitness Log.

Day 4

HONESTY

Value

Honesty means to tell the truth even when it is difficult.

Abraham Lincoln

Abraham Lincoln was so honest that he was given the nickname "Honest Abe." He was taught to tell the truth when he was young. Lincoln displayed honesty in the many jobs he did throughout his life, including being President of the United States of America. People trusted Lincoln when he told them something. Lincoln knew that it was important to keep his promises and his actions always matched his words, even when it was difficult.

Circle each honest choice and cross out the dishonest one.

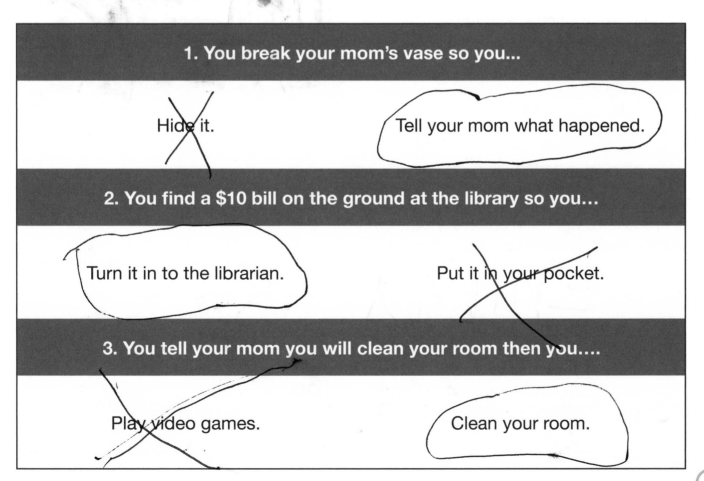

1. You break your mom's vase so you...

Hide it.

Tell your mom what happened.

2. You find a $10 bill on the ground at the library so you...

Turn it in to the librarian.

Put it in your pocket.

3. You tell your mom you will clean your room then you....

Play video games.

Clean your room.

Value: **HONESTY**

Being honest means to be truthful in what you say and do. It means that you do not lie, cheat or steal. Sometimes this can be difficult, especially when we are scared or ashamed about something we did. Sometimes it takes courage to be honest, especially when it is uncomfortable.

> "Whatever you are,
> be a good one"
> -Abe Lincoln

What does honesty look like? Choose an honest action below and draw a picture to represent it in the picture frame.

- I cheat on a test.
- I keep a promise.
- I play fair.
- I take a candy bar from the store without paying.
- I take money out of my dad's wallet without asking.
- I find $5.00 at the library and take it to the front desk.

HONESTY PLEDGE

I promise to tell the truth every day. I will be honest in what I do and what I say.

Emma

My Signature

 How does it feel when someone lies to you?

Sad

 Day 5

 Choose a **Play** or **Exercise** Activity!

Summer Explorer
Discover New Things to Play and Do!

- Visit the library and get a card if you do not have one.

- Make a fort out of blankets and sheets.

- Make a biodegradable bird feeder and hang it in the yard.

- Have a lemonade stand get your friends to help.

- Play flashlight tag.

- Visit a fire station. Does your family have a plan of what to do in case of fire? Plan a family fire drill.

- Sign up for a free summer reading program at your local bookstore.

- Go for a walk.

- Look up and find figures in the clouds.

- Play an outdoor game like "Simon Says" or "Kick the Can" with family or friends.

- Go for a bike ride.

- Pick up trash around your neighborhood and recycle.

- Find an ant colony. Drop some crumbs and observe what happens. Stay away from fire ants.

- Build a castle or fort out of Legos or blocks.

- Use a recycled plastic bag to create a parachute that will slowly fall to the ground.

- Watch a sunrise or sunset, paint a picture of it.

- Run through the sprinklers.

- Make S'mores and tell ghost stories under the stars.

- Create an obstacle course. Invite your friends and time them to see how fast they complete it.

Biodegradable Birdfeeder

 Collect your supplies: peanut butter, birdseed, oranges, and string for hanging.

 Tie a long string around the pinecone or toilet roll before spreading peanut butter on them and rolling in birdseed. Cut an orange in half, scoop out fruit and fill with birdseed. Attach strings to hang feeder in branch.

 Hang your bird treat in the yard and watch for your feathered friends to come and feast.

Summer Journal I

Write about your favorite outdoor summer activity.

Example: Camping, swimming or biking.

I ride my bike.

Play tno myp

PLAYGROUND

play to rind.

I play wafer

bleono

Nouns

A noun is a person, place or thing. Circle the nouns in each house.

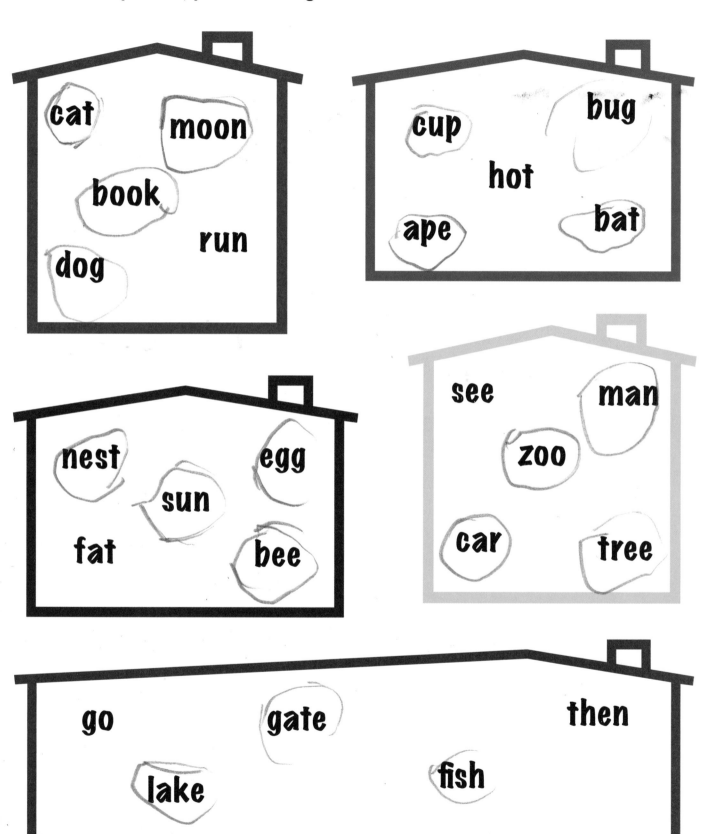

House 1: cat, moon, book, run, dog

House 2: cup, bug, hot, ape, bat

House 3: nest, egg, sun, fat, bee

House 4: see, man, zoo, car, tree

House 5: go, gate, then, lake, fish

When you divide something in half, you divide it into 2 equal parts. Color half of each group.

1.

2.

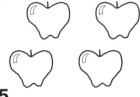

3.

4.

5.

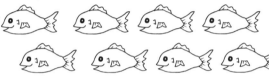

6.

Count by 3s

3, ____6____, 9, ___12___, 15, ___18___, 21, __24__, 27, __30__

What is the value of the coins?

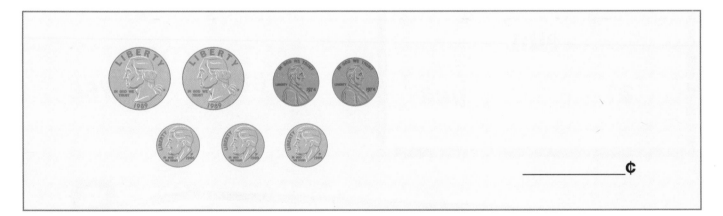

_____ ¢

Choose your **AEROBIC** exercise!

Exercise for today:

Check & Record in Fitness Log.

Day 6

The life cycle of a butterfly has 4 stages: egg, larva, pupa and butterfly. The adult female lays an egg on a leaf. Out of the egg hatches a caterpillar (larva). The caterpillar eats and eats and gets very large. When the caterpillar is done eating it finds a branch or twig and attaches itself. The caterpillar forms a hard shell called a pupa or chrysalis. While in the pupa the caterpillar changes into a butterfly.

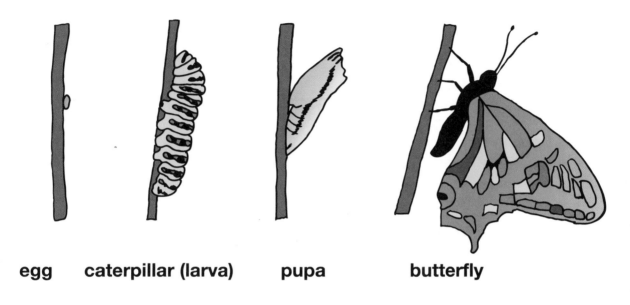

| egg | caterpillar (larva) | pupa | butterfly |

Draw the 4 stages of a butterfly's life cycle and number 1 to 4 in the correct order.

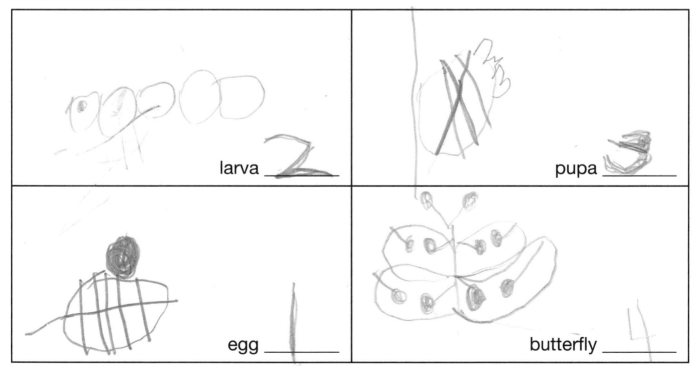

larva _____ 2

pupa _____ 3

egg _____ 1

butterfly _____ 4

 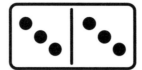 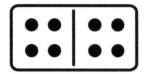

2 + 2 = 4   ___ + ___ = ___   ___ + ___ = ___

___ + ___ = ___   ___ + ___ = ___   ___ + ___ = ___

Draw the other half of each object.

 Choose your STRENGTH exercise!

 Check & Record in Fitness Log.

Exercise for today:

 **Day 7**

_____

Draw a line to match the words to the contractions.

do not

cannot

she is

it is

he is

we are

they will

I have

will not

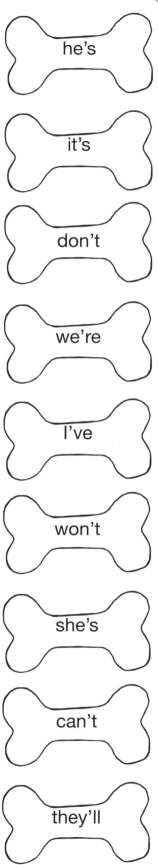

he's

it's

don't

we're

I've

won't

she's

can't

they'll

Time

Write the time.

1. _____ : _____   2. _____ : _____   3. _____ : _____   4 _____ : _____

5 _____ : _____   6 _____ : _____   7 _____ : _____   8 _____ : _____

9. Follow the directions.

first   second   third   fourth   fifth   sixth   seventh   eighth   ninth   tenth

Color the second star yellow.

Underline the fourth star.

Color the tenth star red.

Circle the eighth star.

Cross out the seventh star.

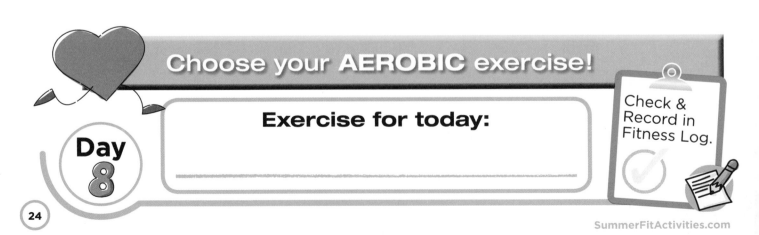

Choose your AEROBIC exercise!

Exercise for today:

Check & Record in Fitness Log.

Day 8

24

SummerFitActivities.com

Long Vowels Using Vowel, silent e

Day
9

Fill in the missing vowels to complete the words. a   e   i   o   u

1. c ___ ke

2. m ___ le

3. k ___ te

4. r ___ pe

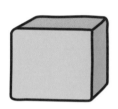

5. c ___ be

6. b ___ ke

7. r ___ ke

8. n ___ s ___

Add silent e to these short vowel words to make them long.

9. not   not + e = _____

10. can   can +e = _____

11. tub   tub + e = _____

12. pin   pin + e = _____

Draw a line to the name of each 3D shape.
Follow the directions to color.

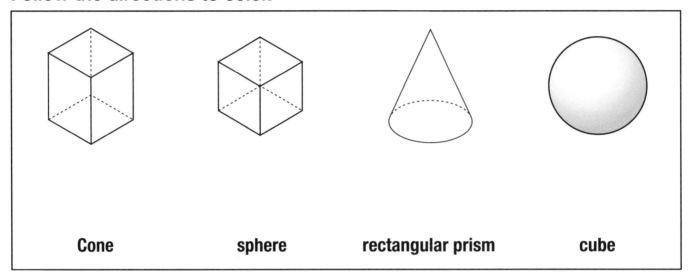

Cone   sphere   rectangular prism   cube

Color the cube blue.   Color the rectangular prism green.

Color the sphere red.   Color the cone yellow.

Color 1/3	Color ½	Color 1/4

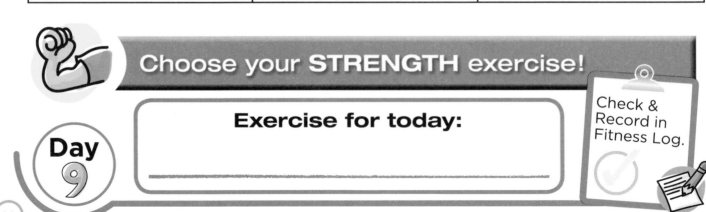

Choose your **STRENGTH** exercise!

Exercise for today:

Check & Record in Fitness Log.

Day 9

COMPASSION

Compassion is caring about others.

A Mother to All

Mother Teresa helped many sick and poor people in India. She took care of people who had nobody else to care for them and gave them safety and a place to live. Mother Teresa sacrificed everything so she could help others, and her actions inspired other people to give to the poor. Mother Teresa won the Nobel Peace Prize for helping people that nobody else wanted to help.

Use these words to fill in the blank.

compassion   poor   others   cared

Mother Teresa showed_____.

Mother Teresa fed the _____.

The Golden Rule says to treat _____the way you want to be treated.

Mother Teresa _____about everyone.

Value: COMPASSION

Having compassion means showing kindness, caring and a willingness to help others who may be sick, hurt, poor, or in need. When you have compassion you are putting yourself in someone else's shoes and really feeling for them. You can do this in very small ways for example when your friend trips and falls. You can do this in larger ways when someone you know does not have enough food to eat.

> "Love and compassion are necessities not luxuries. Without them, humanity cannot survive."
> – Dalai Lama

Unscramble the letters to reveal the traits of being a Hero of Compassion.

dnik

ufltuhgtoh

aricgn

udantnesinrgd

epilngh

ielgnsnti

rstceandoei

ronfmoicgt

avber

tpaenti

Make a "Compassion Jar". Cut out several slips of paper and write on each a way to show compassion. For example: Hold the door for someone, smile at a stranger, or read to a younger child. Choose one to do each day.

(kind) (thoughtful) (caring) (understanding) (helping)
(listening) (considerate) (comforting) (brave) (patient)

Day 10 Choose a **Play** or **Exercise** Activity!

INCENTIVE CONTRACT CALENDAR

My parents and I agree that if I complete this section of

and read _____ minutes a day, my reward will be _____

Child Signature: _____   Parent Signature: _____

Day 1			Day 6		
Day 2			Day 7		
Day 3			Day 8		
Day 4			Day 9		
Day 5			Day 10		

Color the for each day of activities completed.

Color the for each day of reading completed.

Summer Fitness Log

Choose your exercise activity each day from the Aerobic and Strength Activities in the back of the book. Record the date, stretch, activity and how long you performed your exercise activity below. Fill in how many days you complete your fitness activity on your Incentive Contract Calendars.

	Date	Stretch	Activity	Time
examples:	June 4	Run in place	Sky Reach	7 min
	June 5	Toe Touches	Bottle Curls	15 min
1.				
2.				
3.				
4.				
5.				
6.				
7.				
8.				
9.				
10.				

I promise to do my best for me. I exercise to be healthy and active. I am awesome because I am me.

Child Signature: _____

1–2 • © Summer Fit Activities™

Swimming with Verbs

Verbs are words that tell what something or someone does.
They are "action words."

"The shark <u>swims</u>."

Circle the verbs.

run	blue	see	hide	play	dog
swim	sleep	girl	sun	smell	fly

Use the verbs from above to finish the sentences.

1. I like to _____ outside.

2. I _____ the cookies baking.

3. I _____ in my bed.

4. I will _____ my kite.

5. I play _____ and seek.

Write the number:

1. 1 ten = 10

2. 2 tens = _____

3. 3 tens = _____

4. 4 tens = _____

5. 5 tens = _____

6. 6 tens = _____

7. 7 tens = _____

8. 8 tens = _____

9. 9 tens = _____

10. 10 tens = _____

Write the number that is one more.

11. 25 _____

12. 13 _____

13. 36 _____

14. 9 _____

15. 85 _____

16. 99 _____

Write the number that is one less.

17. _____ 15

18. _____ 10

19. _____ 23

20. _____ 51

21. _____ 76

22. _____ 89

Choose your STRENGTH exercise!

Exercise for today:

Check & Record in Fitness Log.

Day 1

A a B b C c D d E e F f G g H h I i

J j K k L l M m N n O o P p Q q R r

S s T t U u V v W w X x Y y Z z

Write the words in alphabetical order.

COLUMN 1	COLUMN 2
cat _____	man _____
fat _____	tan _____
bat _____	fan _____
at _____	pan _____
rat _____	ran _____

1. There were 15 children on the bus. 6 children got off the bus. How many are still on the bus?

15 − 6 = _____

2. There were 10 parakeets and 3 parrots for sale at the pet store. How many birds all together for sale?

10 + 3 = _____

3. Farmer Bob had 12 horses and 6 cows. How many more horses than cows does Farmer Bob have?

12 − 6 = _____

4. Lucy has 4 cousins in Ohio, 7 cousins in Arizona, and 5 cousins in Utah. How many cousins does Lucy have in all?

4 + _____ + _____ = _____

Fill in the missing numbers as you count on.

89, ___, 91, ___, 93, ___, 95, ___, 97, ___, 99, ___, 101, ___,

103, ___, 105, ___, 107, ___, 109, ___, 111, ___, 113, ___, 115, ___

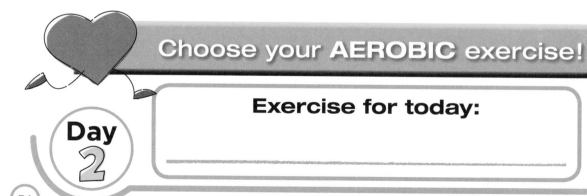

Choose your AEROBIC exercise!

Exercise for today:

Check & Record in Fitness Log.

Day 2

Day 3

Synonyms

Synonyms are words that mean the same or nearly the same thing.
Draw a line to match the synonyms.

happy		sick
Ex.		
leap		same
small		start
keep		chilly
large		jump
begin		glad
alike		angry
cold		silent
mad		tiny
quiet		save
ill		big

1-2 • © Summer Fit Activities™

SummerFitActivities.com

January	31		July	31
February	28		August	31
March	31		September	30
April	30		October	31
May	31		November	30
June	30		December	31

Thirty days has September, April, June, and November.

All the rest have 31. Except February, which has only 28.

1. _____is the first month of the year.

2. The shortest month is_____.

3. _____ is the last month of the year.

4. How many days does April have?_____

5. What month is your birthday in?_____

Choose your STRENGTH exercise!

Day 3

Exercise for today:

Check & Record in Fitness Log.

 **Sequencing**

Number the parts of the stories in the correct order.

1. The bird built its nest. Then the bird laid 3 eggs in the nest. After a while the eggs hatched and the baby birds were hungry. The mother bird fed her babies.

2. Mary and her mother wanted to make a cake. First they got the ingredients they would need. They followed the recipe to make the batter. Mary's mother put the cake in the oven to bake. After an hour the cake was done. That night Mary's family had a birthday party and served the cake. It was delicious!

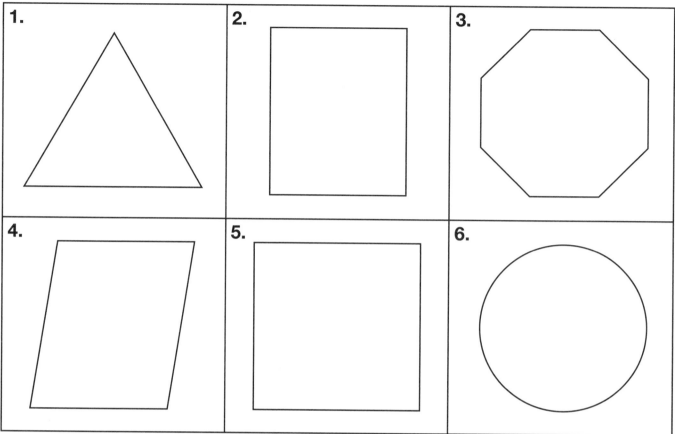

Color the circle green.

Color the parallelogram blue.

Color the octagon orange.

Color the triangle red.

Color the rectangle yellow.

Color the square purple.

7. Which shape has more than 6 vertices (corners)? _____

Choose your AEROBIC exercise!

Exercise for today:

Check & Record in Fitness Log.

Day 4

1-2 • © Summer Fit Activities™

SummerFitActivities.com

Being Trustworthy means keeping your promises.

Value

Harriet Tubman

Harriet Tubman was a slave before the Civil War. She had to work very hard with no pay and was sometimes treated very badly. From the time she was a little girl, Harriet dreamed of freedom and although she was small, she was strong-willed. When she was an adult, Harriet escaped slavery to become free, and she wanted to help others be free. She risked her life many times to lead other slaves to safety and freedom. People trusted her with their lives and she never let them down.

Draw a picture of one way you can be trustworthy at home.

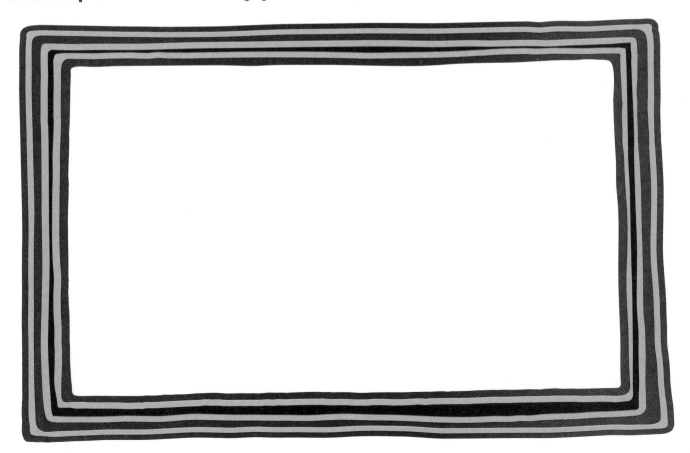

Value: TRUSTWORTHINESS

FAMILY ACTIVITIES

Choose one or more activities to do with your family or friends.

 Talk about ways you show you are trustworthy. Remember that when you are dishonest and not truthful, people will not trust you. Think about the times you have been trustworthy. Write down at least 5 words that describe how you felt being trusted.

 Talk about what it means to be a trustworthy friend. Make a Friendship bracelet and give it to one of your friends. Let them know they can count on you to be a good friend.

 Write down the word TRUSTWORTHY. How many little words can you make from the letters?

VALUES ARE A FAMILY AFFAIR

Read more about
TRUSTWORTHINESS

A Picture Book of Harriet Tubman
By David A. Adler

My Brother the Thief
By Marlene Fanta Shyer

The Bad Times of Irma Baumlein
By Carol Brink

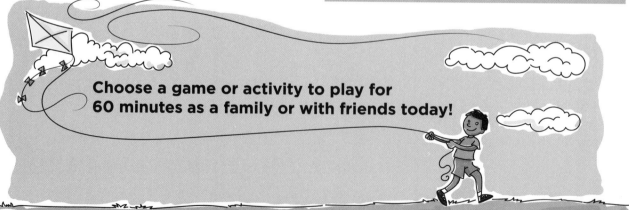

Choose a game or activity to play for 60 minutes as a family or with friends today!

Day 5
Choose a Play or Exercise Activity!

Summer Explorer

Discover New Things to Play and Do!

- Play in the rain. Make mud pies and jump in puddles.

- Have a book exchange with your friends.

- Finger paint.

- Make your own musical instruments out of cardboard boxes and perform a song.

- Create a healthy dinner menu for your family.

- Visit a lake, river, or pond. Bring a notebook to do some nature drawings.

- Make your own bubble solution. Go outside and make some enormous bubbles.

- Pick wildflowers and arrange them in a glass or jar.

- Draw a flipbook.

- Make cookies for a neighbor — deliver them with a parent.

- Go to the park with a friend.

- Sign up for a free project at Home Depot, Lowes, or Michaels.

- Make a scavenger hunt to do with friends or family.

- Plant something: flowers, vegetables, herbs, a tree.

- Read to a younger sibling.

- Make a photo album or scrapbook.

- Try a new cookie recipe.

- Have a water balloon fight.

- Help an elderly neighbor weed his/her garden.

- Paint or draw a self-portrait.

Giant Bubbles

6 cups Water
1/2 cup Dish Soap (Dawn blue)
1/2 cup Cornstarch
1 TBSP Baking Powder
1 TBSP Glycerin
(Glycerin found in cake decoration aisle at craft store)

 Slowly mix together in large bucket or dishpan.

 Let solution sit for 1-2 hours.

 Tie a length of string between two straws to make a bubble wand or use store bought wands. The bigger your wand, the bigger your bubbles!

Summer Journal II

Write about your family vacation.

_____

- -

_____

_____

- -

_____

_____

- -

_____

_____

- -

_____

_____

- -

_____

_____

- -

_____

Plurals are words that mean more than one. Plurals are made by adding "s" or "es."

Dog   **Dogs**

| singular | plural |

Read the plural words. Write the singular form.

cars _____   balls _____

boxes _____   trucks _____

shirts _____   foxes _____

girls _____   dresses _____

When words end with a "y," we change the "y" to an "i" and add "es."
Cross out the "y" and add "ies." Write the new word.

baby _____

bunny _____

story _____

guppy _____

1-2 • © Summer Fit Activities

1 ten 0 ones = 10

1 ten + 1 one = 11

_____ ten _____ ones = _____

_____ ten _____ ones = _____

_____ ten _____ ones = _____

_____ ten _____ ones = _____

_____ tens _____ ones = _____

_____ tens _____ ones = _____

_____ tens _____ ones = _____

_____ tens _____ ones = _____

Choose your **AEROBIC** exercise!

Exercise for today:

_____

Day
6

Check & Record in Fitness Log.

What doesn't belong?

Asking and telling sentences.

Change each asking sentence to a telling sentence.

What is the dog playing with?

Example: The dog is playing with a ball.

_____

1. Is it warm today?

_____

2. Is the boy riding the bike?

_____

3. Does the number three come after two?

_____

Telling sentences end in a period (.). Asking sentences end in a question mark (?). Add the correct punctuation mark to each sentence.

4. Are you going to swim _____

5. My fish is orange _____

6. Are the birds in the tree _____

7. She is baking a cake _____

1. Finish writing the tally marks. Count by 5's to 100.

5   10   _____   _____   _____

_____   _____   _____   _____   _____

_____   _____   _____   _____   _____

_____   _____   _____   _____   _____

Add.

2.	2	3.	4	4.	5	5.	3	6.	1
	3		2		1		3		2
	+1		+2		+2		+3		+5

 Choose your STRENGTH exercise!

 Check & Record in Fitness Log.

Exercise for today:

 **Day 7**

 **Amazing Adjectives**

Adjectives are words that describe a noun. Read the sentences and circle all the adjectives.

1. The (blue) bird perched in the (tall) tree.

2. The slimy little worm inched its way across the wet, gray rock.

3. The fast, spotted dog chased the striped cat across the big yard.

4. The soft, orange cat purred while it slept in the warm sun.

5. I watched the tiny bug crawl under the wrinkled, green leaf.

6. We like to swim in the cool lake on a hot day.

Think of two adjectives to describe each noun.

7. _____ , _____ fish

8. _____ , _____ boy

9. _____ , _____ book

10. _____ , _____ frog

11. _____ , _____ house

12. _____ , _____ cupcake

This table shows all the pets of the children in Mrs. Bell's class. Count how many of each pet.

dogs _____	
cats _____	
birds _____	
fish _____	
crabs _____	
turtles _____	

1. Which pet is most popular?_____

2. How many more dogs are there than crabs? _____

3. Which pet lives in water? _____

4. Which pet is there only 1 of? _____

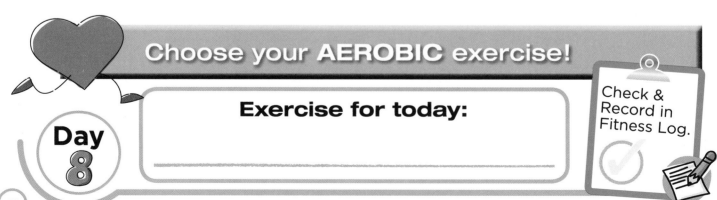

Choose your AEROBIC exercise!

Exercise for today:

Check & Record in Fitness Log.

Day 8

Compound Words

Compound words are bigger words made by two smaller words put together. Add the smaller words together to make a compound word and write the word on the line. Draw a picture for the new word.

Ex. pan + cake = pancake

1. bird + house = _____

2. snow + man = _____

3. foot + ball = _____

4. fire + man = _____

5. cup + cake = _____

Look at the picture. Write the 2 words that make up the compound word.

6. = butter + fly

7. = _____ + _____

8. = _____ + _____

9. = _____ + _____

1. Does the dotted line show a line of symmetry? Yes or No?

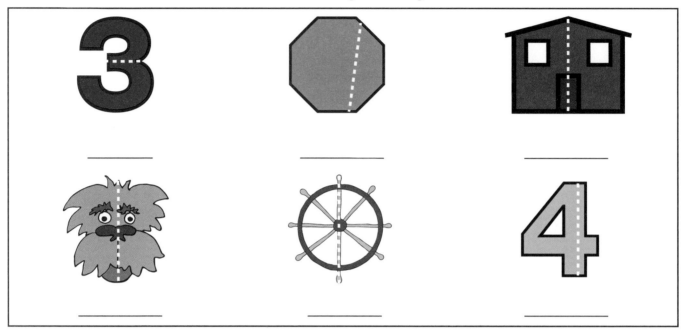

2. Draw a line of symmetry through each shape.

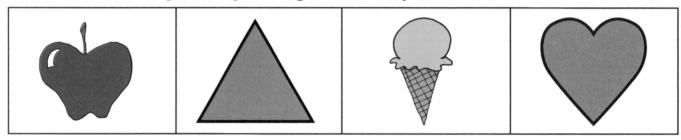

3. Draw the other half of each symmetrical shape.

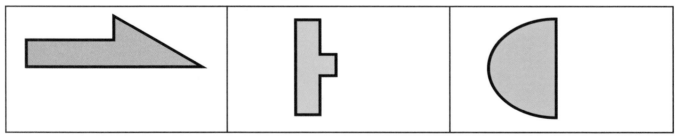

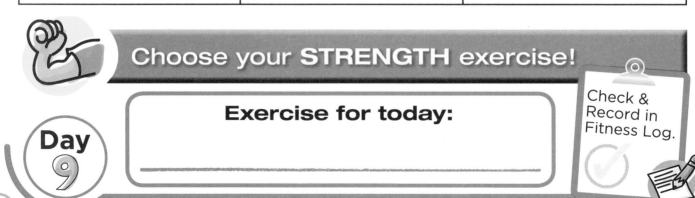

Choose your **STRENGTH** exercise!

Exercise for today:

Check & Record in Fitness Log.

Day 9

SELF-DISCIPLINE

Value

Self-discipline is to have control of your actions.

Stephanie Lopez Cox works hard to reach her goals. Her focus and dedication helped her gain a spot on the U.S. National Women's Soccer Team that won gold in the Olympics. Stephanie practices very hard and is committed to doing things that will help her be the best athlete she can be. Stephanie is dedicated to bettering the world around her, and is committed to helping children in foster care because she grew up with foster siblings.

Self-discipline means self-control. Make good choices.

Stephanie practices hard to be the best soccer player she can be. She also works hard to be the best person she can be by helping others. Write down what Stephanie does to help others. Draw a picture.

_____

_____

_____

_____

_____

_____

_____

Value: SELF-DISCIPLINE

FAMILY ACTIVITIES

Choose one or more activities to do with your family or friends.

Let's talk about it...

Encourage your child to be determined and focused when completing a task or project. Identify a project or sport that your child has not done such as swimming, playing basketball, or tennis. Introduce him/her to it and encourage them to stay involved for a certain amount of time.

 Plan to exercise together as a family this week. Have a family walk after dinner. Choose an activity to do together. Hike, bike, swim, dance and play together. At night, play a game of "flashlight tag." Whoever gets "tagged" by the light is "it."

 Give up TV for a day, a week, or longer. Instead, spend time outside, reading, or with family and friends.

 Plan a sequence of events or activities to do in one day. Before you move on to the next one you must finish the one before it.

VALUES ARE A FAMILY AFFAIR

Read more about SELF-DISCIPLINE

Greedy Greeny
By Jack Gantos

A Chair for my Mother
By Vera B. Williams

Oh, the Places You'll Go!
By Dr. Seuss

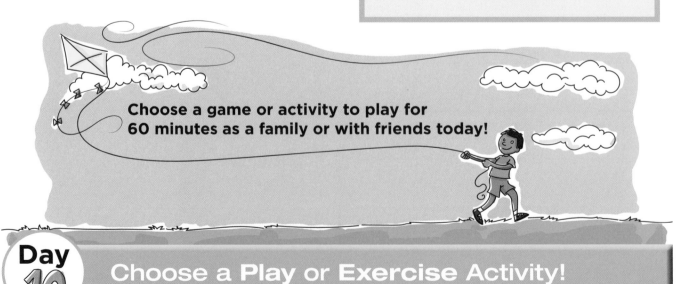

Choose a game or activity to play for 60 minutes as a family or with friends today!

Day 10
Choose a **Play** or **Exercise** Activity!

INCENTIVE CONTRACT CALENDAR

My parents and I agree that if I complete this section of

Summer Fit Activities™

and read _____ minutes a day, my reward will be _____

Child Signature: _____   Parent Signature: _____

Day 1			Day 6		
Day 2			Day 7		
Day 3			Day 8		
Day 4			Day 9		
Day 5			Day 10		

Color the for each day of activities completed.

Color the for each day of reading completed.

Summer Fitness Log

Choose your exercise activity each day from the Aerobic and Strength Activities in the back of the book. Record the date, stretch, activity and how long you performed your exercise activity below. Fill in how many days you complete your fitness activity on your Incentive Contract Calendars.

	Date	Stretch	Activity	Time
examples:	June 4	Run in place	Sky Reach	7 min
	June 5	Toe Touches	Bottle Curls	15 min
1.				
2.				
3.				
4.				
5.				
6.				
7.				
8.				
9.				
10.				

I promise to do my best for me. I exercise to be healthy and active. I am awesome because I am me.

Child Signature: _____

An ant is an insect. It has six legs and a three-part body. Ants use their antennae to find food. They smell and feel with their antennae. Ants live and work together in a colony. Every colony has a queen. The queen's job is to lay the eggs. The other ants are worker ants, nursery ants, and soldier ants.

In an anthill there are many rooms and tunnels, all made by the busy ants. Some rooms are used to store food, while other rooms are used for eggs and the ants that have just hatched. Ants are very strong and can carry up to 50 times their weight.

head
abdomen
thorax
eyes
antennae
legs

Label the parts of the ant.

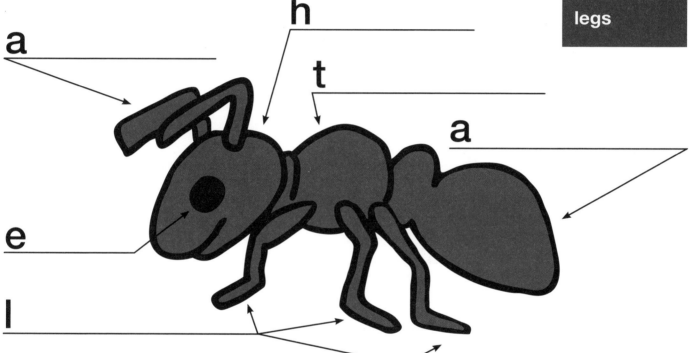

h _____

a _____

t _____

a _____

e _____

l _____

Circle the correct answer and write it in the blank.

1. The eggs are laid by the _____.	queen	soldier ants
2. Ants are _____.	weak	strong
3. What do ants use to find food?	ears	antennae
4. How many legs to ants have?	6	8

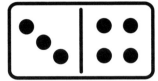
Write 2 addition problems shown by each domino.

1. Ex. 	2. 
3 + 4 = 7	2 + _____ = _____
4 + 3 = 7	_____ + 2 = _____
3.	4. 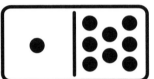
_____ + _____ = _____	_____ + _____ = _____
_____ + _____ = _____	_____ + _____ = _____

What would you add to each number to make a 10?

Ex. 1 + 9 = 10	3 + ___ = 10	2 + ___ = 10
4 + ___ = 10	6 + ___ = 10	9 + ___ = 10
5 + ___ = 10	7 + ___ = 10	8 + ___ = 10

Choose your **STRENGTH** exercise!

Check & Record in Fitness Log.

Day 1

Exercise for today:

_____

SummerFitActivities.com

Sentence Mix-Up

Write each mixed up sentence correctly. Remember to capitalize the first word and don't forget the period.

the mat on the cat is

Ex. <u>The cat is on the mat.</u>

1. a man a bag of sand had

_____

2. swim day I can all

_____

3. cheese mouse the ate the

_____

4. Exclamatory sentences show strong feelings and end with exclamation marks. Circle the exclamation mark(s) in each sentence.

Help! The snake is out!	Oh no! I broke the glass!
Get the dog!	Ow! That pot is hot!
Wow! That cat is fast!	Look out!

Measurement

Circle the unit of measurement you would use to measure each item.

1.

Inches   miles

2.

gallons   inches

3.

miles   pounds

4.

ounces   pounds

5.

inches   pounds

6.

inches   miles

7.

ounces   inches

8.

inches   miles

9.

ounces   pounds

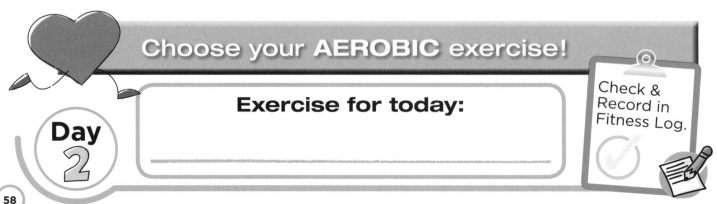

Choose your AEROBIC exercise!

Exercise for today:

Check & Record in Fitness Log.

Day 2

Antonyms are words that have opposite meanings. Draw a line to connect the antonyms.

Ex. up   under

strong   slow

fast   down

over   dirty

in   short

clean   out

tall   weak

Choose an antonym from the word box to replace the underlined word in each sentence.

open	stop	messy	truth	always

1. Please <u>shut</u> the window. _____

2. Your room is very <u>clean.</u> _____

3. You should always tell the <u>lie</u>. _____

4. <u>Never</u> say please and thank you. _____

5. A red light means <u>go</u>. _____

Mark >, <, or =

1.Ex. 4 + 1 **<** 5 + 2	2. 3 + 4 _____ 2 + 3	3. 5 + 5 _____ 3 +7
4. 4 + 4 _____ 2+ 1	5. 9 – 5 _____ 5 + 2	6. 6 – 2 _____ 3 + 2
7. 7 + 5 _____ 14 - 2	8. 8 + 3 _____ 12-2	9. 1 +1 _____ 2 + 0

Practice making a 10 and adding on.

Ex. 8 + 2 + 3 = 13

10. 9 + 7 + 1 = _____	13. 5 + 6 + 10 = _____
11. 5 + 2 + 5 = _____	14. 8 + 5 + 10 = _____
12. 7 + 6 + 3 = _____	15. 4 + 8 + 9 = _____

Count by 10's (adding on 10) to finish the pattern.

70, ___, 90, ____, 110, ____, 130, ____, 150, ____, 170, ____, 190, ____, 210 ____

Choose your STRENGTH exercise!

Exercise for today:

Day 3

Check & Record in Fitness Log.

Fill in the missing letters "oa" or "ee" to complete the word.

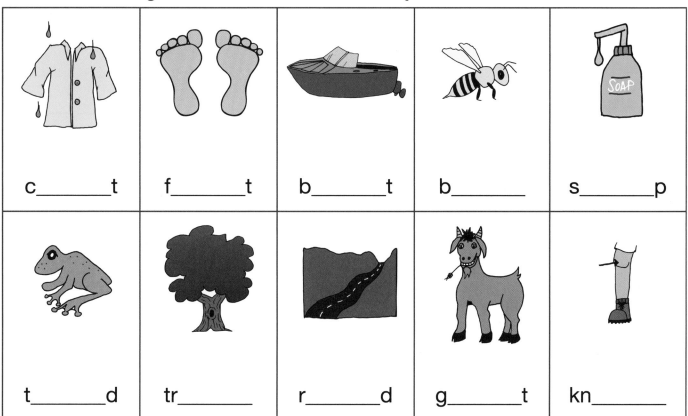

c_____t f_____t b_____t b_____ s_____p

t_____d tr_____ r_____d g_____t kn_____

Circle the correctly spelled word in each row.

1. som	some	summ
2. weant	wint	went
3. know	knowe	knoew
4. abowt	aboute	about
5. howse	house	hous

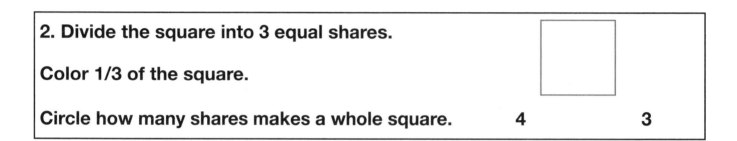

1. Divide the circle into two equal shares.

Color ½ of the circle.

Circle how many shares makes a whole circle. 2 1

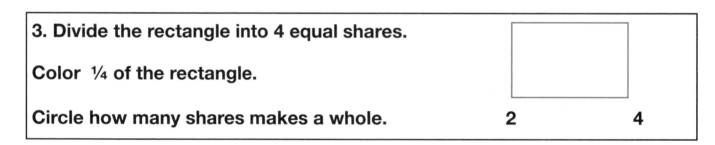

2. Divide the square into 3 equal shares.

Color 1/3 of the square.

Circle how many shares makes a whole square. 4 3

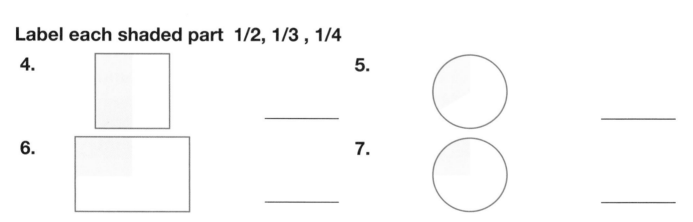

3. Divide the rectangle into 4 equal shares.

Color ¼ of the rectangle.

Circle how many shares makes a whole. 2 4

Label each shaded part 1/2, 1/3 , 1/4

4.

5. _____

6. _____

7. _____

Choose your **AEROBIC** exercise!

Exercise for today:

Day 4

Check & Record in Fitness Log.

62

1-2 • © Summer Fit Activities™

KINDNESS

Kindness is being nice and caring about other people, animals and the earth.

PELE

Pele is from Brazil and is said to be one of the best soccer players to ever play the game. He amazed fans on the soccer field with his tricks and many goals. Pele loved and helped people around the world. He had a big heart and a big smile. He was kind to everyone, especially children. He wanted them to have a chance to follow their dreams too.

Color the hearts showing ways of being kind. Write 3 more ways.

Tell someone they are special

Pick up something someone has dropped

Kindness starts with me

Call your Grandparents and tell them you love them

Hold the door open for someone

Value:

KINDNESS

FAMILY ACTIVITIES

Choose one or more activities to do with your family or friends.

 Play "10 good things" with your friends or family. Pick a person and tell 10 nice things about them.

 Write notes to your neighbors thanking them for being good neighbors.

 Have a lemonade stand and donate the money you earn to a food bank or homeless shelter.

 Collect toys, books, and games you no longer play with and donate them.

Let's talk about it...

Children learn what they live, if they see you practicing random acts of kindness, they will want to do them too. Discuss things your family can do together to help others. Set aside some time to volunteer at a soup kitchen or homeless shelter. Remind your child that kindness begins with a smile and should be practiced at home too!

VALUES ARE A FAMILY AFFAIR

 Read more about **KINDNESS**

The Kindness Quilt
By Nancy Wallace

Jamaica Tag - Along
By Juanita Havill

The Elves and the Shoemaker
By Paul Galdone

Choose a game or activity to play for 60 minutes as a family or with friends today!

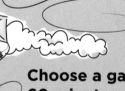

Day 5

Choose a **Play** or **Exercise** Activity!

1-2 • © Summer Fit Activities™

SummerFitActivities.com

Summer Explorer

Discover New Things to Play and Do!

- Learn how to make paper airplanes.

- Host a board game night.

- Play charades.

- Use cardboard boxes to build an outdoor house, fort, train, or pirate ship.

- Play jump rope, marbles, or hopscotch.

- Use "junk" from around your house to create an art masterpiece.

- Make some puppets and put on a puppet show.

- Go through your toys and have a toy exchange or donate to charity.

- Fly a kite.

- Draw with sidewalk or paint with water on the cement.

- Create a new exercise or exercise routine.

- Organize a neighborhood garbage walk to pick up trash and clean up your neighborhood.

- Search for animal tracks. How many can you identify?

- Play in the sand. Build a sand castle.

- Play Frisbee.

- Write a letter to someone and mail it.

- Visit a local nature preserve.

- Make a robot or other creation out of items from your recycle bin.

- Paint a pet rock.

Recyclable Creations "Junk Monsters"

 Gather clean cans, bottles, and boxes from recycling bin.

 Use plastic lids, newspaper strips, nuts, screws, buttons, pipe cleaners, rubber bands to make faces, and arms and legs. Your parents will need to help you glue with a hot glue gun.

 Create monsters, robots, or your family members!

Summer Journal III

Write about your best friend, brother or sister.

_____

- -

_____

_____

- -

_____

_____

- -

_____

_____

- -

_____

_____

- -

_____

_____

- -

_____

Solid, Liquid, or Gas?

Matter

Look around and you will see matter everywhere. Matter is anything that has weight and takes up space. It is anything made of atoms and molecules. Matter can be sorted in three states: solid, liquid, and gas. Water can be in all three states as ice, water, and steam.

Label the pictures below as solid, liquid, or gas.

1. _____

2. _____

3. _____

Answer.

4. Matter is anything that has weight and takes up _____.

5. The three stages of matter are _____,

_____, and_____.

6. Write S for solid, L for liquid, and G for gas to describe each word.

rock _____

air _____

chair _____

milk _____

honey _____

steam _____

Color one square for each item shown in the picture.

carrots										
cornstalks										
lettuce										
tomatoes										
squash										
pumpkins										
	1	2	3	4	5	6	7	8	9	10

1. **How many carrots and tomatoes altogether?** _____ + _____ = _____

2. **How many more heads of lettuce than squash?** _____ - _____ = _____

3. **How many corn and heads of lettuce together?** _____ + _____ = _____

Choose your **AEROBIC** exercise!

Exercise for today:

Check & Record in Fitness Log.

Day 6

68

Mind Your Manners!

Good manners are important and help us get along with others. Answer the questions using the words from the list.

please	thank you	hello	may
nice	open	excuse me	sorry

1. Greet people with a _____ and a smile.

2. When you meet someone new, you say, " _____ to meet you."

3. When you make a mistake you say, "I am _____ ."

4. Hold the door _____ for people.

5. It is polite to say "_____ ," when someone gives you a gift.

6. Say "_____ ," when you bump in to someone.

7. When you ask for something, you should say "_____ ."

8. When you ask permission to do something, you say, "_____ I, please?"

Unscramble the letters to make a manners word.

esplae _____   sxecue em _____

htkna oyu _____   yma I _____

Count the coins to find the cost of each item. Write the amount on the line.

1. _____¢

2. _____¢

3. _____¢

4. _____¢

5. **Ann had .60¢. She bought an apple for .30¢.**
How much does she have left?

_____¢ - _____¢ = _____¢

6. **A single scoop of ice cream costs .40¢.**
Sierra bought 2 scoops. How much did it cost?

_____¢ + _____¢ = _____¢

Choose your STRENGTH exercise!

Day
7

Exercise for today:

_____

Check & Record in Fitness Log.

Needs and Wants

Needs are things we have to have to live a healthy life. Wants are things we would like but are not necessary.

Circle the needs, cross off the wants.

Name three needs:			
Name three wants:			

1.

10 – 8 = _____	8 + _____ = 10	12 – 4 = _____
4 + _____ = 12	7 + _____ = 11	11 – 3 = _____
10 + 5 = _____	15 – 5 = _____	13 + 1 = _____

2. Write the number that is one less than each of these.

_____ 50	_____ 14	_____ 21	_____ 8
_____ 26	_____ 37	_____ 76	_____ 10

3. Write the number that is one more than each of these.

12 _____	22 _____	29 _____	34 _____
60 _____	112 _____	100 _____	105 _____

4. Write the number that is 10 more than each of these.

20 _____	40 _____	10 _____	30 _____
70 _____	50 _____	90 _____	80 _____

Choose your AEROBIC exercise!

Exercise for today:

_____

Check & Record in Fitness Log.

Day 8

1-2 • © Summer Fit Activities™

Classifying

Cross out the object in each group that does not belong.

1.

2.

3.

4.

5.

6.

7.

8.

9.

How many tens and ones in each number?

1. 22 _____ tens _____ ones	4. 19 _____ tens _____ ones
2. 34 _____ tens _____ ones	5. 85 _____ tens _____ ones
3. 59 _____ tens _____ ones	6. 70 _____ tens _____ ones

Order the numbers from least to greatest.

7. 19, 12, 16 _____ , _____ , _____	9. 49, 47, 43 _____ , _____ , _____
8. 33, 13, 23 _____ , _____ , _____	10. 60, 16, 96 _____ , _____ , _____

11. Count on by 2's to fill in the missing numbers.

2, _____, 6, _____, 10, _____, 14, _____, 18, _____, 22, _____, 26, _____, 30

Choose your STRENGTH exercise!

Day 9

Exercise for today:

_____

Check & Record in Fitness Log.

1-2 • © Summer Fit Activities™

SummerFitActivities.com

COURAGE

Courage means doing the right thing even when you are feeling scared.

Rosa Parks

Rosa Parks was one of the heroes of the Civil Rights Movement in the United States of America. Before the Civil Rights Movement, African-Americans were not treated well. They had to sit in the back of busses and even had to give up their seat to white people. One day after work, Rosa got on the bus to go home. When the bus driver told Rosa to give up her seat for a white man she refused. Rosa showed courage by standing up for what was right even though she was afraid.

Circle the correct answer(s).

Rosa was asked to give up her _____ .   purse   seat

Rosa was supposed to sit at the back
of the bus because she was _____ .   black   a woman

Rosa showed she had _____ .   tired feet   courage

Rosa stood up for what was
right for _____ .   herself   herself and others

Value: COURAGE

FAMILY ACTIVITIES

Choose one or more activities to do with your family or friends.

 As a family, watch a movie that demonstrates courage such as *Charlotte's Web*, *The Sound of Music*, *The Wizard of Oz*, *The Lion King*, *ET*, or *Finding Nemo*. Discuss how the characters in the movie display courage. What might have happened if they hadn't been courageous?

 Make and decorate a pennant for your room that says "I believe in myself." Discuss with your parents how being the best you can be is an act of courage.

 Talk about the courage it takes for a blind person to get through the day. Take turns blindfolding each other and try to do your everyday things. Ask your parents to help you look up the story of Ben Underwood, a blind teen who rides a skateboard and plays video games.

 Think about the most courageous person you know. Write about how they demonstrate courage.

Let's talk about it...

Courage is something built over time. Discuss everyday situations with your child and the opportunities they have to be brave. Read books about people who display courage. Encourage them to share their fears and brainstorm together ways to face and overcome those fears. Talk with them about a time you were afraid but found the courage to get through.

VALUES ARE A FAMILY AFFAIR

Read more about COURAGE

Brave Irene
By William Steig

If a Bus Could Talk:
The Story of Rosa Parks
By Faith Ringgold

Sheila Rae, the Brave
By Kevin Henkes

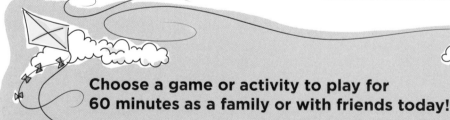

Choose a game or activity to play for 60 minutes as a family or with friends today!

 Day 10

Choose a Play or Exercise Activity!

INCENTIVE CONTRACT CALENDAR

My parents and I agree that if I complete this section of

Summer Fit Activities™

and read _____ minutes a day, my reward will be _____

Child Signature: _____   Parent Signature: _____

Day 1			Day 6		
Day 2			Day 7		
Day 3			Day 8		
Day 4			Day 9		
Day 5			Day 10		

Color the for each day of activities completed.

Color the for each day of reading completed.

Summer Fitness Log

Choose your exercise activity each day from the Aerobic and Strength Activities in the back of the book. Record the date, stretch, activity and how long you performed your exercise activity below. Fill in how many days you complete your fitness activity on your Incentive Contract Calendars.

	Date	Stretch	Activity	Time
examples:	June 4	Run in place	Sky Reach	7 min
	June 5	Toe Touches	Bottle Curls	15 min
1.				
2.				
3.				
4.				
5.				
6.				
7.				
8.				
9.				
10.				

I promise to do my best for me. I exercise to be healthy and active. I am awesome because I am me.

Child Signature: _____

Abbreviations

Abbreviations are shortened words. Abbreviations usually begin with a capital letter and end with a period. Match each word with its abbreviation.

Word		Abbreviation
Doctor		Jan.
Mister		Sun.
Inches		Nov.
Street		Fri.
Feet		Aug.
January		In.
Sunday		Dr.
Wednesday		Mr.
August		Tues.
October		Ft.
Friday		Sat.
February		Sept.
Saturday		Oct.
Tuesday		Feb.
September		Wed.
November		St.

Make 2 correct number sentences using addition.

1.	2.
_____ + _____ = _____	_____ + _____ = _____
_____ + _____ = _____	_____ + _____ = _____

3. There were 8 frogs sitting on a log. 3 frogs jumped into the pond. How many frogs are left on the log? Why?

_____ frogs are left because _____ - _____ = _____

Make 2 correct number sentences using subtraction.

12   8   4
4. _____ - _____ = _____   5. _____ - _____ = _____

3   9   6
6. _____ - _____ = _____   7. _____ - _____ = _____

Choose your STRENGTH exercise!

Exercise for today:

Check & Record in Fitness Log.

Day 1

Community Helpers

There are many people in our communities who help us.
Solve the riddle by writing in the correct community helper on the line.

teacher	doctor	grocer	police officer
dentist	mail carrier	bus driver	firefighter

1. I deliver your mail and packages through rain or shine.

Who am I? _____

2. I make sure you stay healthy and help when you feel sick.

Who am I? _____

3. I keep the market stocked with healthy food for you to eat.

Who am I? _____

4. I work at school and help you learn to read, write and add.

Who am I? _____

5. I clean your teeth and make sure they stay healthy and strong.

Who am I? _____

6. I fight crime and help keep you safe in your community.

Who am I? _____

7. I help put out fires and rescue people who are in trouble.

Who am I? _____

Write the numeral.

1. fourteen _____	6. five _____
2. ten _____	7. twelve _____
3. eight _____	8. eleven _____
4. fifteen _____	9. three _____
5. seven _____	10. zero _____

11. Draw the hands to show the time.

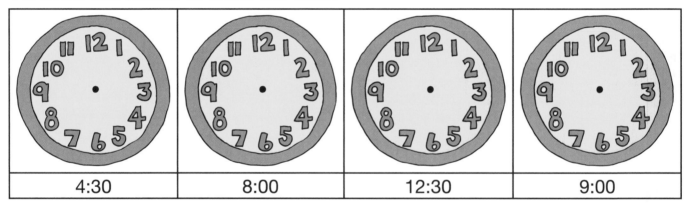

4:30	8:00	12:30	9:00

12. Count on by 3 to finish the pattern.

3, _____, 9, _____, 15, _____, 21, _____, 27, _____ .

Choose your **AEROBIC** exercise!

Exercise for today:

Check & Record in Fitness Log.

Day 2

1-2 • © Summer Fit Activities™

SummerFitActivities.com

Words and Sounds

Fill in with "ch" or "sh" to complete each word.

_____ eep   _____ eese   _____ icken   _____ irt

_____ oe   fi _____   pea _____   _____ ip

Change the asking sentences into telling sentences.

1. Are we going to the beach?

_____

2. Is the ball in the tree?

_____

Change the telling sentences into asking sentences.

3. The ship is sailing across the sea.

_____

4. You can climb the peach tree.

_____

This is a map of Franklin Park.

1. If you walk from the trees to the play structure, which direction do you go?

_____

2. Where can you feed the ducks? _____

3. What is east of the pond? _____

4. What is the name of this park? _____

5. To go from the pond to the dog park you would walk _____

6. Circle the balloon cart.

Choose your STRENGTH exercise!

Day 3

Exercise for today:

Check & Record in Fitness Log.

Geography - On the Map

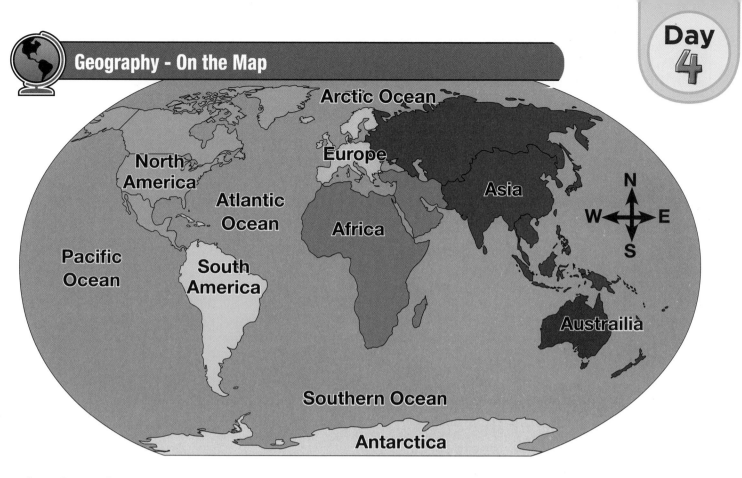

Look at the map and answer the questions.

A continent is a large body of land. The United States is in North America. There are seven continents and five oceans on Earth.

Name the five oceans.

1. _____   2. _____

3. _____   4. _____

5. _____

6. What continent is Canada and the United States on? _____

7. What is the biggest continent? _____

8. What continent is south of Asia? _____

9. What continent is east of South America? _____

10. What continent is north of Africa? _____

Look at each shape, write the name of the line and count the number of sides and vertices. A vertex is a corner, the point where 2 sides meet.

pentagon	rectangle	octagon	triangle

1.

_____

_____ sides

_____ vertices

2.

_____

_____ sides

_____ vertices

3.

_____

_____ sides

_____ vertices

4.

_____

_____ sides

_____ vertices

5. Add 3 more triangles to make a rectangle.

6. Can you name a shape that has no flat sides and no vertices? _____

Choose your AEROBIC exercise!

Check & Record in Fitness Log.

Exercise for today:

Day 4

RESPECT

Respect is being nice to yourself and to others.

Mahatma Gandhi

Mahatma Gandhi was born on October 2, 1869. He was a gentle boy while growing up and became a strong and respected leader in India. Gandhi taught that if you hurt someone else you are also hurting yourself. He showed people how to accept each other even if they were different. He believed there would be peace in the world if everyone would respect and accept each other.

Fill in the blanks to complete the sentences.

Mahatma Ghandi was known as the Father of I ___ ___ ___ ___.

He believed in peace not w ___ ___.

Ghandi said if you h ___ ___ ___ someone else, you hurt yourself.

Ghandi wanted all people to r ___ ___ ___ ___ ___ ___ each other.

Value: RESPECT

Respect is showing good manners and acceptance of other people and our planet. Respect is celebrating differences in culture, ideas and experiences that are different than yours. Respect is accepting that others have lessons to teach us because of their experiences.

"Be the change you want to see in the world."

- Mahatma Gandhi

List 3 ways to show respect to your parents and teachers.

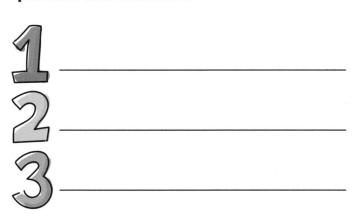

1 _____

2 _____

3 _____

We can disrespect people with our words. Remember to THINK before we speak. Ask yourself...

T = is it true?

H = Is it helpful or hurtful?

I = Is it inspiring?

N = Is it necessary?

K = Is it kind?

WAYS TO SHOW RESPECT

Respect the Earth.
Collect items to recycle.

Respect a different culture:
Listen to some music or try a new food that is associated with a culture or belief that is different than yours.

Day 5 Choose a **Play** or **Exercise Activity!**

Summer Explorer

Discover New Things to Play and Do!

- Learn the phases of the moon. Look at it several nights in a row and see if you can recognize the various phases.

- Make up a song or dance.

- Have a yard sale.

- Start a rock collection.

- Have a potluck with family and friends.

- Visit a farmers market. Learn about the origin of the food you eat.

- Volunteer.

- Take a hike.

- Have a neighborhood softball game.

- Make popsicles.

- Grab some binoculars and go on a bird watching hike.

- Go camping.

- Have a western theme night. Wear bandannas and your cowboy boots, and roast hotdogs. Try line dancing or watch an old Western.

- Go on a nature walk. Collect twigs, leaves, pebbles, and shells. Glue them on card stock to make a 3D masterpiece.

- Help a neighbor by mowing their lawn or weeding.

- Draw a comic strip.

- Bake cookies and take some to a friend or neighbor.

- Play Hide and Seek.

- Have a pillow fight.

- Create a time capsule.

Nature Walk

 Go on a nature walk in a field, park or beach.

 Collect grass, twigs, shells, pebbles, etc.

 Arrange your finds inside a cardboard box, glue down to create a 3D masterpiece.

Summer Journal IV

Write about your best summer day so far.

**Homophones**

Homophones are words that sound the same. They have different spellings and different meanings. Read each sentence and write the correct homophone to complete the sentence.

1. I saw the _____ land on the flower.	(be, bee)
2. My sister is _____ years old.	(too, to, two)
3. The summer _____ is hot.	(sun, son)
4. The _____ rode away on his horse.	(knight, night)
5. When we were camping we saw a _____ in the forest.	(bare, bear)
6. I got a new _____ of shoes for my birthday.	(pear, pair)
7. My _____ tickles just before I have to sneeze.	(nose, knows)
8. Please _____ me at the park after lunch.	(meet, meat)
9. There are many fish in the _____ .	(see, sea)
10. I have _____ brothers.	(for, four)

Solve each problem. Watch the signs.

1.　56
　　－ 24

2.　42
　　＋ 14

3.　84
　　－ 40

4.　29
　　－ 13

5.　72
　　＋ 14

6.　68
　　－ 32

7.　53
　　＋ 25

8.　11
　　－ 10

9. Circle the numbers that are even.

8	12	10	13	21
6	7	22	4	16

10. Circle the numbers that are odd.

3	5	10	40	13
7	11	8	15	77

Choose your AEROBIC exercise!

Exercise for today:

Check & Record in Fitness Log.

Day 6

My Family Tree

With your parent's help fill in this family tree. Add the names of your parents, siblings and grandparents.

_____
_____

_____   _____   _____
_____   _____   _____
_____   _____   _____
_____   _____   _____

Grandparents   _____   Grandparents

                               Siblings

                           _____

                               Me

_____   _____
Father   Mother

I have numbers that are important to me. Fill out the numbers that help tell about you. Ask your parents if you need help.

My birthdate is _____ .

My phone number is _____ .

My street address is _____ .

My parent's cell-phone number is _____ .

I am _____ years old.   My name has _____ letters in it.

I have _____ people in my family.

Draw the hands on the clock to show the time. Write the time.

I wake up at :   _____:_____

I have lunch at:   _____:_____

I go to bed at:   _____:_____

 Choose your **STRENGTH** exercise!

Check & Record in Fitness Log.

Day 7

Exercise for today:

1-2 • © Summer Fit Activities™

 **Pronouns**

Pronouns are words that can take the place of nouns. Use a pronoun to complete each sentence.

he	she	it	they
her	them	him	we

1. Mom likes to bake. _____ makes tasty cookies.

2. Gabe and John like to play ball. _____ are on the soccer team.

3. Grace and I are going to the park. _____ will go on the swings.

4. The balloon got stuck in the tree. _____ popped.

5. Noah got some cars for his birthday. _____ played with _____ all day.

6. Jane was late and missed _____ bus.

7. I am going to visit my grandparents. I will stay with _____ for a week.

1. Draw a line from each alien to the spaceship that is 10 less.

2. Circle the bank with the most money.

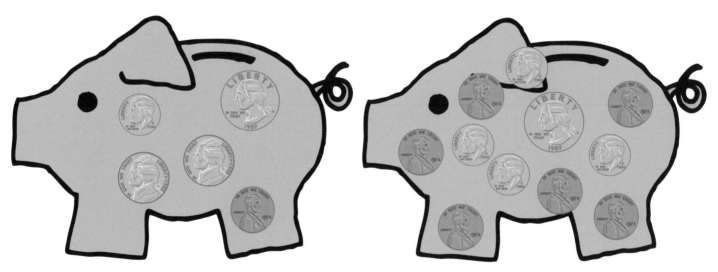

Choose your AEROBIC exercise!

Exercise for today:

Day 8

Check & Record in Fitness Log.

1-2 • © Summer Fit Activities™

SummerFitActivities.com

Creepy, crawly

Eating healthy food will make me strong.

Foods that are good for me can be divided into 4 groups: breads and grains, meats and protein, vegetables and fruits, and milk and cheese (dairy).

Circle the healthy foods. Cross off the foods that are not healthy.

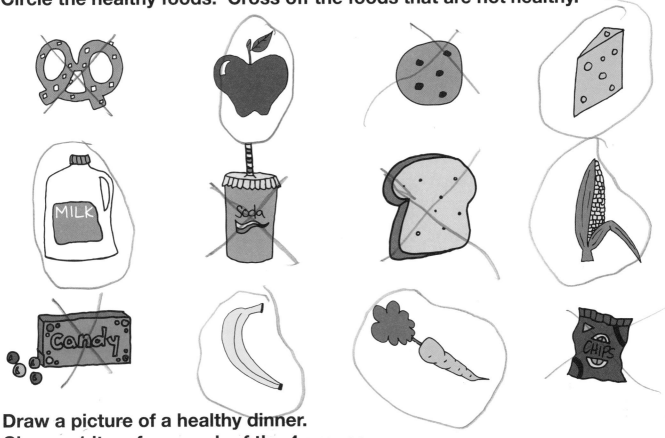

Draw a picture of a healthy dinner.
Choose 1 item from each of the 4 groups.

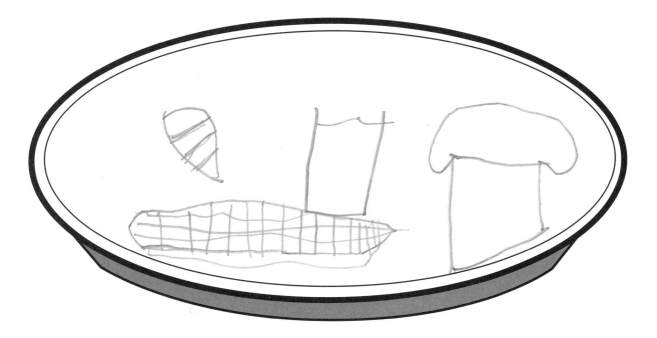

1.	The name of this 3D shape is.	cube	cylinder
	Can this shape roll?	yes	no
	Can you stack this shape?	yes	no
2.	The name of this 3D shape is.	cone	pyramid
	Can this shape roll?	yes	no
	Can this shape be stacked?	yes	no
3.	The name of this 3D shape is.	cylinder	cone
	Can this shape roll?	yes	no
	Can you stack this shape?	yes	no
4.	The name of this 3D shape is.	cube	sphere
	Can this shape roll?	yes	no
	Can this shape be stacked?	yes	no

5. Draw a pentagon.	**6. Draw a hexagon.**

7. Color the pattern and write your pattern rule.

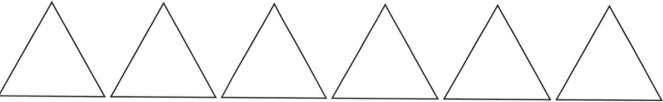

Write your pattern rule:_____

 Choose your STRENGTH exercise!

Day 9

Exercise for today:
_____

Check & Record in Fitness Log.

98

1–2 • © Summer Fit Activities™

RESPONSIBILITY

Responsibility is to do the things you know that you should.

Terrance Stanley Fox was a very good athlete. His favorite sport was basketball but he also played rugby, golf and ran cross country in high school. Sadly, Terry lost one of his legs because he got cancer. He felt it was his responsibility to do all that he could for other people with cancer. Even though it was very hard, he set off to run across Canada with an artificial leg to raise money for cancer research. He called his run the Marathon of Hope. When he started to run not many people knew about Terry or what he was doing but now people all over the world participate or take part in an event named after Terry to raise money for cancer research.

Circle the end of the sentences that show responsibility.

Mom tells me to remember my lunch so I....

| leave it on the counter. | remember to take my lunch. |

I threw my ball through the neighbor's window so I....

| go right away and admit what I did. | run away. |

I ride my bike to the park so I....

| wear my helmet. | leave my helmet at home. |

Mom tells me to clean my room so I....

| hide everything under the bed. | put my things away and clean my room. |

Value: RESPONSIBILITY

You can show responsibility in many different ways. From doing your homework to babysitting your little brother or sister to helping someone else who is in need, being responsible is being accountable for your actions. Big and small, choosing what you do with your time and efforts is an important part of being responsible.

> "I am not doing the run to become rich or famous."
>
> - Terry Fox, *Marathon of Hope*

Monday	
Tuesday	
Wednesday	
Thursday	
Friday	
Saturday	
Sunday	

Build or set up a bird feeder in your yard and be responsible for feeding the birds. Use the chart below to track how many birds you feed for a week.

 We are all responsible for the environment. Watch one of these family movies and talk about how being irresponsible can affect the environment. Movies: *Over the Hedge, Hoot, Free Willy, Bambi, Fern Gully, The Last Rainforest,* or *Happy Feet.*

Day 10

Choose a **Play** or **Exercise** Activity!

1-2 • © Summer Fit Activities™

INCENTIVE CONTRACT CALENDAR

My parents and I agree that if I complete this section of

Summer Fit Activities™

and read _____ minutes a day, my reward will be _____

Child Signature: _____   Parent Signature: _____

Day 1			Day 6		
Day 2			Day 7		
Day 3			Day 8		
Day 4			Day 9		
Day 5			Day 10		

Color the for each day of activities completed.

Color the for each day of reading completed.

Summer Fitness Log

Choose your exercise activity each day from the Aerobic and Strength Activities in the back of the book. Record the date, stretch, activity and how long you performed your exercise activity below. Fill in how many days you complete your fitness activity on your Incentive Contract Calendars.

	Date	Stretch	Activity	Time
examples:	June 4	Run in place	Sky Reach	7 min
	June 5	Toe Touches	Bottle Curls	15 min
1.				
2.				
3.				
4.				
5.				
6.				
7.				
8.				
9.				
10.				

I promise to do my best for me. I exercise to be healthy and active. I am awesome because I am me.

Child Signature: _____

Magnets

Magnets only attract certain items. Not all metals are attracted to magnets. Look at the pictures below. Circle the items you think a magnet would attract, cross off the items the magnet will not attract.

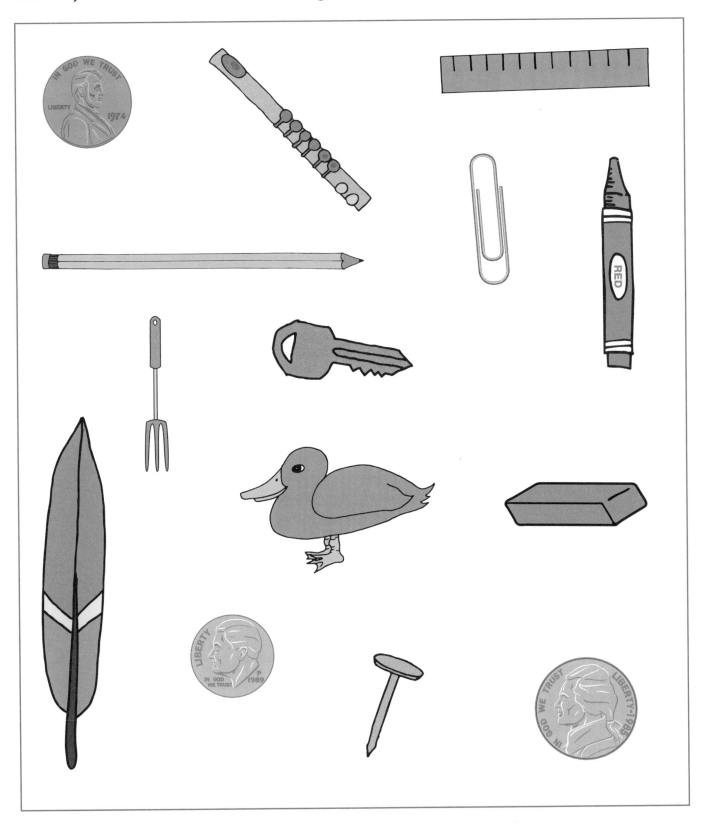

Mixed Practice

Draw a line to match the measurements.

1. 1 hour   16 ounces

2. 1 yard   12 months

3. 1 minute   60 minutes

4. 1 year   3 feet

5. 1 pound   60 seconds

Write the sums to complete the equations.

6. 6 + 2 + 3 = _____   7. 7 + 1 + 3 = _____   8. 8 + 2 + 4 = _____

How much money? Circle the greater amount.

9.

= $_____

10.

= $_____

Choose your STRENGTH exercise!

Check & Record in Fitness Log.

Exercise for today:

Day 1

Read the following fable from Aesop and answer the questions below.

The Dog and the Shadow

A dog, crossing a bridge over a stream with a piece of meat in his mouth, saw his own shadow in the water and took it for that of another dog, with a piece of meat double his own in size. He immediately let go of his own, and fiercely attacked the other dog to get his larger piece from him. He thus lost both: that which he grasped at in the water, because it was a shadow; and his own, because the stream swept it away.

1. What did the dog see in the water below? _____

2. The dog let go of his piece of meat so he could get a _____

piece of meat.

3. Circle the word you might use to describe the dog?

kind   greedy   sick

4. What is the moral or lesson of this story? _____

_____

5. Draw a picture to illustrate this story.

1. Write half of each number.

½ of 10 = _____

½ of 12 = _____

½ of 14 = _____

½ of 16 = _____

½ of 18 = _____

½ of 20 = _____

2. Color the even numbers purple and the odd numbers yellow.

3. Write + or – to get the correct answer.

6 _____ 4 = 10

10 _____ 5 = 5

8 _____ 3 = 11

12 _____ 6 = 6

Choose your **AEROBIC** exercise!

Exercise for today:

Check & Record in Fitness Log.

Day 2

1-2 • © Summer Fit Activities™

Following directions.

Write numbers 1–5 to put the directions in the right order.

1. _____Get your toothbrush and toothpaste.

_____Put everything away.

_____Rinse your toothbrush.

_____Put toothpaste on your toothbrush.

_____Brush your teeth.

2. _____Put on a stamp.

_____Mail the letter.

_____Address the envelope.

_____Write the letter and seal it in the envelope.

_____Get paper, envelope and a stamp.

Data Management

Look at the Venn diagram showing which children in Mrs. Clark's class like green apples and which ones like red apples.

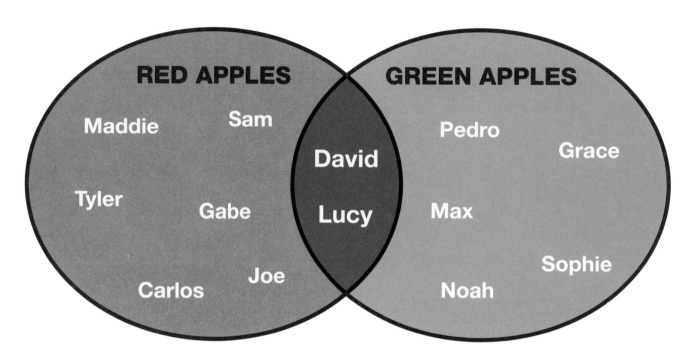

RED APPLES

Maddie   Sam

Tyler

Gabe

Carlos   Joe

David

Lucy

GREEN APPLES

Pedro

Grace

Max

Sophie

Noah

1. Which students like red apples? _____

_____ .

2. Which students like green apples? _____

_____ .

3. Which students like both red and green apples? _____

_____ .

Choose your STRENGTH exercise!

Exercise for today:

Check & Record in Fitness Log.

Day 3

There are many different types of animals.

MAMMALS are warm blooded animals that have fur and give birth to live young. Most mammals live on land.

BIRDS have feathers and wings and most can fly. Birds have beaks but no teeth and hatch from eggs.

REPTILES can live on land and in water. They are cold blooded and most hatch from eggs.

INSECTS have 6 legs, three body parts and hatch from eggs. Most insects can fly.

Write the animal names in the correct column.

eagle	grasshopper	lizard	tiger	robin	monkey
fly	turtle	snake	owl	ladybug	dog

Mammals	Birds	Reptiles	Insects

1.

_____ hundreds

_____ tens

_____ ones

What is the number? _____

2.

_____ hundreds

_____ tens

_____ ones

What is the number? _____

Circle the digit in the ones place.

Ex. 4⃝6	17	38	50
93	62	125	89

Circle the digit in the tens place.

Ex. ⃝5 9	23	10	35
87	139	94	48

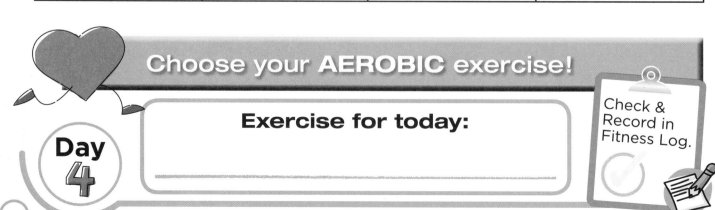

Choose your AEROBIC exercise!

Exercise for today:

Check & Record in Fitness Log.

Day 4

PERSEVERANCE

Perseverance is trying again and again and not giving up.

Shark Attack!

Bethany Hamilton was sitting on her surfboard one sunny day in Hawaii, waiting for the next big wave. Suddenly a shark attacked her and she was left without her arm. Thirteen-year old Bethany survived and was soon surfing again. Getting back in the water meant overcoming her fear of another attack and learning to surf again with only one arm. Bethany kept at it and persevered by never giving up on her dreams even when they seemed impossible.

Perseverance

Fill in the blanks using the words from the box below.

surf	dreams	shark	fear	arm

Bethany was attacked by a _____. She lost her _____.

Bethany overcame her _____.

She learned to _____ again.

Bethany never gave up on her _____.

Value:

PERSEVERANCE

FAMILY ACTIVITIES

Choose one or more activities to do with your family or friends.

 As a family, tackle a big job you have been putting off such as cleaning the garage or painting the fence. Work together as a family to persevere and finish the job. Celebrate with ice cream to emphasize the sweet satisfaction of a job well done.

 People with disabilities face many obstacles each day. Read about Helen Keller and her perseverance in overcoming her blindness and deafness. Put on a blindfold and imagine how hard it would be to go about your day without your sight. What can you do? What can't you do?

 Farmers need perseverance and a lot of patience when planting their crops. One bad storm or drought can destroy everything they have worked for. Plant a small vegetable garden and take care of weeding and watering it. Be patient and your perseverance will pay off.

VALUES ARE A FAMILY AFFAIR

Read more about PERSEVERANCE

D. W. Flips
By Marc Brown

Pancakes for Breakfast
By Tommie DePaola

Katie and the Big Snow
By Virginia L. Burton

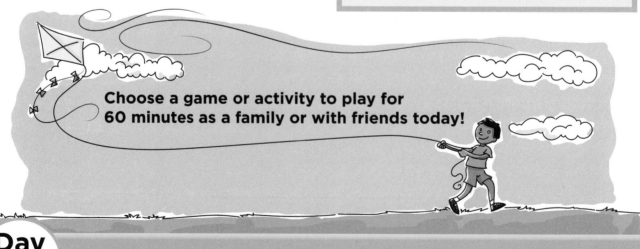

Choose a game or activity to play for 60 minutes as a family or with friends today!

Day 5
Choose a **Play** or **Exercise** Activity!

Summer Explorer
Discover New Things to Play and Do!

- Make up a secret handshake.

- Play "I spy".

- Write a poem.

- Make a telescope out of paper towel tubes. Have a family stargazing night: How many constellations can you find? Can you find the Big Dipper? Polaris?

- Do a puzzle.

- Make ice cream.

- Make a friendship bracelet and give it to a friend.

- Learn to fold Origami.

- Go fishing.

- Camp in the backyard.

- Learn how to juggle.

- Feed the ducks.

- Turn on some music and dance.

- Hang butcher paper on a wall and paint a mural.

- Learn the alphabet in sign language.

- Learn Pig Latin.

- Host a tea party.

- Have a Super Hero Day - dress like your favorite super hero or make up your own. Dress up your pet!

- Walk a dog.

- Do a science experiment.

- Pretend you are a reporter. Interview someone special and write an article about him/her.

Stargazing

 Collect paper towel tubes.

 Gather your family on a clear night to stargaze through your "telescopes".

 Look for The Big Dipper, Cancer and other star constellations.

Summer Journal V

Write about your favorite pet or animal.

_____

- -

_____

_____

- -

_____

_____

- -

_____

_____

- -

_____

_____

- -

_____

 **Vowel Sounds**

Day 6

Fill in the missing letters "oa" or "ou" to complete each word.

b_____t   h_____se   c_____t

s_____p   h_____nd   t_____d

m_____se   r_____d   g_____t

Read these sight words to an adult.

when	about	easy
about	could	never
from	know	soon
away	where	much
been	much	again
after	take	does
there	were	always

SummerFitActivities.com

Match the coins with object they will buy.

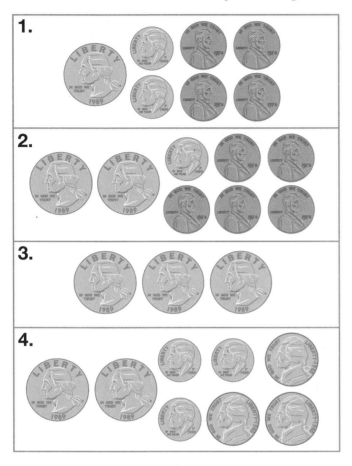

1.

2.

3.

4.

75¢

95¢

65¢

49¢

5. Jasmine has these coins. Which coin does she need to make a dollar?

_____

6. Jose bought a cookie for .35 cents, he paid with $1.00. How much change does he have?

_____

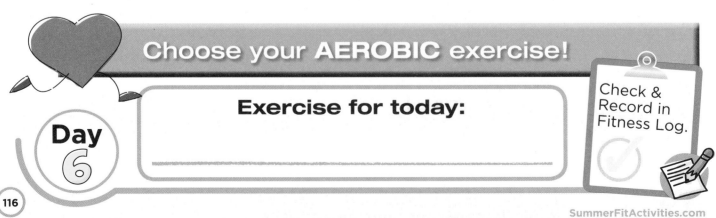

Choose your **AEROBIC** exercise!

Exercise for today:

Day 6

Check & Record in Fitness Log.

1-2 • © Summer Fit Activities™

SummerFitActivities.com

Unscramble the mixed up letters to make words of what you might see at the beach. Then draw a line from the word to its picture.

sand castle	sunglasses	pail	ball
waves	starfish	shovel	umbrella

1. liap _____

2. snusglases _____

3. labl _____

4. murbllea _____

5. evwas _____

6. snda cstela _____

7. trassfih _____

8. hsvole _____

Color 1 equal part. Circle the name of the part you colored.

1. 1/4   1/3   1/2

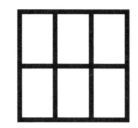

2. 1/4   1/5   1/6

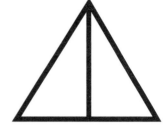

3. 1/3   1/2   1/4

Write the before and after numbers by 5s.

4. _____ 25 _____	5. _____ 15 _____
6. _____ 80 _____	7. _____ 130 _____

Write the before and after numbers by 10's

8. _____ 50 _____	9. _____ 75 _____
10. _____ 145 _____	11. _____ 90 _____

Order these numbers from least to greatest.

12.   180,   108,   80,   188,   118

_____,   _____,   _____,   _____,   _____

Day 7

Choose your STRENGTH exercise!

Exercise for today:

_____

Check & Record in Fitness Log.

SummerFitActivities.com

Busy as a Beaver

Busy as a Beaver

Beavers are interesting animals. They are dark brown and usually weigh between 30 and 60 pounds. The beaver's tail is very thick and is shaped like a large paddle at the end. Beavers have huge front teeth and only eat plants, bark from trees, and twigs. Beavers are excellent swimmers and live in streams and lakes with trees nearby. They spend their time cutting tree limbs and branches with their teeth. They drag branches to the site of their lodge, where they make a stick and mud dam. Beavers have only one mate, and live together in families.

Fill in the blank with the correct word to finish the sentence.

lodge	paddle	brown
streams	plants and trees	dam

1. The color of most beavers is _____.

2. Beavers have huge front teeth and like to eat

_____ and _____.

3. A beaver's house is called a _____.

4. A beaver has a thick tail shaped like a _____.

5. Beavers live in lakes and _____.

6. Beavers use sticks, branches and mud to build a

_____.

Write the correct number on the line.

Ex. 1. 536 = 500 + 30 + 6	5. 129 = ____ + 20 + 9
2. 748 = 700 + 40 + ____	6. 646 = 600 + ____ + 6
3. 352 = ____ + 50 + 2	7. 523 = 500 + 20 + ____
4. 159 = 100 + ____ + 9	8. 145 = ____ + 40 + 5

Write the number that is the same as the word.

9. one hundred, four tens, three ones = ____ ____ ____

10. five hundreds, two tens, six ones = ____ ____ ____

Look at the three digits.

2   8   5

11. Using the three digits, make the greatest number you can. _____

12. Using the three digits, make the smallest number you can. _____

Choose your AEROBIC exercise!

Exercise for today:

Check & Record in Fitness Log.

Day 8

Read the paragraph about a special day.

Saturday was a special day for me. My dad and I went to a baseball game. Dad and I found our seats right behind home plate. The stadium was full of people. The smell of popcorn, peanuts, and hotdogs filled the air.

When the first batter hit a home run we all cheered and jumped up in our seats. People were blowing horns, clapping, and yelling! Our team won the game and I felt proud. I had a great time at the game with my dad.

To Do: Think about a special day. Write words in the web to describe your day.

smell:

see:

"My Day"

hear:

taste:

feel:

Write a paragraph that tells about your special day. Use the words from your web.

_____

_____

_____

_____

_____

_____

_____

Fill in the blanks with the correct answer.

1. An hour is _____ minutes.

4. A dozen is _____.

2. A year is _____ months.

5. A minute is _____ seconds.

3. A day is _____ hours.

6. A foot is _____ inches.

7.
```
    45
    22
  + 32
  _____
```

8.
```
    35
    12
  + 52
  _____
```

9.
```
    54
    21
  + 23
  _____
```

10.
```
    24
    64
  + 40
  _____
```

11. Paulo went to the swimming pool at 2:00 and went home at 5:00.

How many hours was he at the pool? _____

12. What day of the week is between Monday and Wednesday?

_____

13. What is 100 more than 452? _____

14. What is 100 more than 176? _____

15. How many days are there in a year? _____

Choose your STRENGTH exercise!

Exercise for today:

Check & Record in Fitness Log.

Day 9

Friendship is spending time with someone else that you care about — animals or people!

Value

KARTICK

Kartick grew up in India near Bannerghatta National Park where he learned to love animals. At night he would go into the park and watch wild animals drink water from fresh pools under the moonlight. He showed them respect and did not scare them off by being loud. He grew to love them very much and cared for their safety. He considered them to be his friends. When he was older, Kartick helped rescue an elephant named Raju from captivity. Raju cried because she was so happy.

Kartick uses different things to watch and protect his animal friends. Draw a line from each picture to its name.

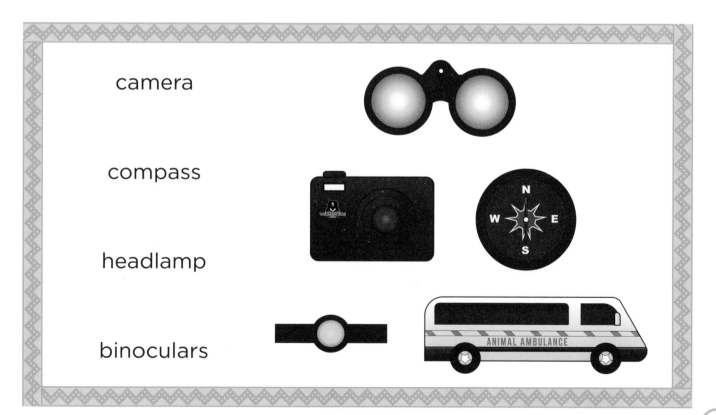

camera

compass

headlamp

binoculars

Value:

FRIENDSHIP

"Don't walk behind me; I may not lead. Don't walk in front of me; I may not follow. Just walk beside me and be my friend."

– Winnie the Pooh

```
H O N E S T W S Q M M H B E T O H L
P K K P K H U C V C Z S E R U D R U
G D X D O O C P P B H N U F E M S F
W A K W R Y R F I A G D V A Z D Q T
F U V E L O P D N J I V C A O S Y C
E G N M K L Y U O K L P E K W J R E
Y E L K K L I E H H O Q H H O O T P
G I J I K T D S U T Y Z Z C T M W S
E K N B A P Y K T J A M R D O Z B E
N D C U W T P X U E L L P W B G K R
Z R Y B W L M B K S N N R Q Z D B H
X R G G U F Q J S R P P S T K I M V
G W V C U K B D R Z W N N V G T A B
U P G J G K L D G X U T H B R I C I
Y I A F Q S X S U I B P R L L H E P
K N I P F B J Y D M R K U O J T Q P
```

Find the words below that are qualities of a good friend.

WORD BANK

fun	listen
loyal	generous
honest	respectful
kind	

Be a Good Friend

 Invite a friend over. Let them choose what to play first.

 Watch *Toy Story* with your family. Talk about how the characters in the movie portray true friendship.

 Make a friendship bracelet for one of your friends. Give it to them and tell them why you are happy to be friends.

 **Day 10**

Choose a **Play** or **Exercise** Activity!

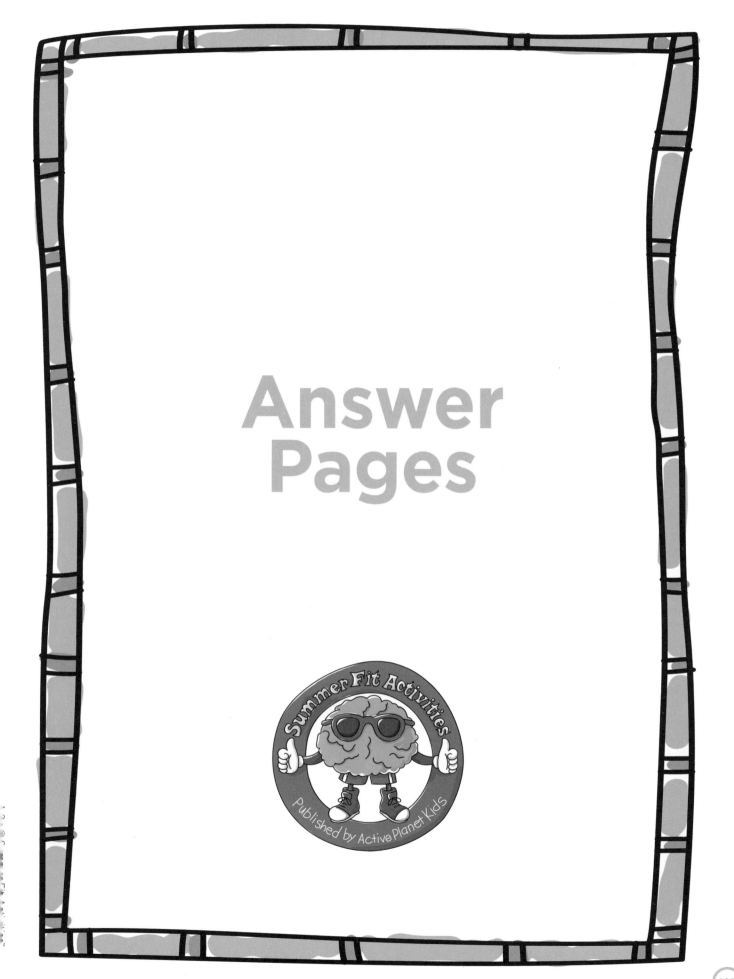

Answer Pages

Answer Key

Summer Skills Review

Math
1. 7,10,8,2,5,4.
2. 3:00, 9:30
3. 8 + 5 =13, 13 – 5=8
4. 6,8,10,12;19,21,23,25;36,38,40 ,42.
5. <,>,=
6. 43,62,27.
7. 11, 5th star circled
8. Square, triangle.
9. 25,10,5,1.
10. 7 dogs, 5 cats.
11. March
12. 9-3 =6
13. Đ circle colored.
14. 4,8,12,16,20.
15. 9,15
16. 20,40,60,80,100.

Reading
1. Sat, bat, mat; men, hen, den.
2. Cat, tree, rabbit, day.
3. Boy, bike, park.
4. I, we, his.
5. Mary, Utah, Maple, Street.
6. My bike has a flat tire.
7. Ride,swim.
8. Read words.

p. 7:
ug, at, op, ee, un, og, ig, en,
ree, oat, at, oat, tar, op, eet, ar.
1. cat   2. tree
3. star   4. boat

p. 8:
1. 2   2. 8   3. 1
4. 3   5. 6   6. 3
7. 8   8. 10
9. 2 quarters or quarter, 2 dimes and a nickel.
10. 2 dimes, 1 nickel.
11. 4,8,12,16,20

p. 9:
circled items: boy with ball, boy with dog, apple, swimmer, toothbrush, bike

p. 10:
1. 4   2. 1   3. 2
4. 3   5. 5

p. 11:
1. L   2. S   3. S
4. L   5. L   6. S
7. S   8. S   9. S
10. L   11. S   12. S
13. S   14. L

p. 12:
1. on time   2. early   3. late.
4. 6:00   5. 3:00   6. 5:30
10,20,30,40,50,60,70,80,90,100.

p. 13:
1. blossom   2. leaf
3. seedling   4. stem
5. roots.

p. 14:
<,>,<,>
circle, circle, square, triangle.

p. 15:
1. Tell your mom what happened
2. Turn it in to the librarian.
3. Clean your room.

p. 19:
cat, moon, book, dog;
cup, ape, bug, bat;
nest, sun, egg, bee;
zoo, man, car, tree;
gate, lake, fish.

p. 20:
1. 3 ants   2. 2 apples
3. 5 stars   4. 1 dog
5. 4 fish   6. 6 hearts
6,12,18,24,30. .82 cents.

p. 21:
larva 2, pupa 3,
    egg 1, butterfly 4.

p. 22:
3 + 3 = 6, 4 + 4 = 8,
6 + 6 = 12, 1 + 1 =2, 5 + 5=10
other half of each object.

p. 23:
don't, can't, she's, it's, he's,
we're, they'll, I've, won't.

p. 24:
1. 5:00   2. 3:00   3. 12:30
4.6:00   5. 9:30   6. 4:00
7. 2:30   8. 10:00

p. 25:
1. a   2. u   3. i
4. o   5. u   6. i
7. a   8. o,e.
9. note, cane, tube, pine

Correct work every day or two to help keep students accountable. This also shows your child you are interested in their work.

Answer Key

p. 26:

rectangular prism, cube, cone, sphere. 1/3 colored, 1/2 colored, 1/4 colored.

p. 27:

compassion, poor, others, cared.

p. 31:

circled words: run, swim, sleep, see, hide, play, smell, fly.

1. play   2. smell   3. sleep
4. fly   5. hide.

p. 32:

1. 10	2. 20	3. 30
4. 40	5. 50	6. 60
7. 70	8. 80	9. 90
10 . 100	11. 26	12. 14
13. 37	14. 10	15. 86
16. 100	17. 14	18. 9
19. 22	20. 50	21. 75
22. 88		

p. 33:

Column 1: at, bat, cat, fat, rat.
Column 2: fan, man, pan, ran, tan.

p. 34:

1. 9   2. 13   3. 6
4. 16

90, 92, 94, 96, 98, 100, 102, 104, 106, 108, 110, 112, 114, 116.

p. 35:

leap/jump, small/tiny, keep/save, large/big, begin/start, alike/ same, cold/chilly, mad/angry, quiet/ silent, ill/sick.

p. 36:

1. January   2. February
3. December   4. 30
5. answers vary.

p. 37:

1. 4, 1, 3, 2 2. 4, 1, 3, 2.

p. 38:

1. red   2. yellow   3. orange
4. blue   5. purple   6. green
7. octagon.

p. 39:

Answers vary.

p. 43:

car, box, shirt, girl, ball, truck, fox, dress, babies, bunnies, stories, guppies.

p. 44:

1 ten 2 ones = 12,
1 ten 3 ones = 13,
1 ten 4 ones = 14,
1 ten 5 ones = 15,
2 tens 0 ones = 20,
2 tens 1 ones = 21,
3 tens 2 ones = 32,
4 tens 3 ones = 43,
4 tens 4 ones = 44.

p. 45:

1. It is warm today.
2. The boy is riding the bike.
3. The number three comes after two.
4. ?   5. .
6. ?   7. .

p. 46:

15, 20, 25, 30, 35, 40, 45, 50, 55, 60, 65, 70, 75, 80, 85, 90, 95, 100.
2. 6   3. 8   4. 8
5.9   6.8

p. 47:

1. blue, tall
2. slimy, little, wet, gray.
3. fast, spotted, striped, big.
4. soft, orange, warm.
5. tiny, wrinkled, green.
6. cool, hot.
7-12. answers vary.

p. 48:

8 dogs, 7 cats, 4 birds, 5 fish, 3 crabs, 1 turtle.
1. dogs   2. 5
3. fish   4. turtle.

p. 49:

1. birdhouse   2. snowman
3. football   4. fireman
5. cupcake   6. butter + fly
7. air + plane   8. hay + stack
9. water + melon.

p. 50:

yes, no, yes, yes, yes, no.
2. line drawn through each shape equally.
3. other half of each shape drawn.

p. 51:

Stephanie helps children in foster care. Picture varies.

Reward well done and completed work with stickers, stamps or hand written messages.

Answer Key

p. 55:

antennae, head, thorax, abdomen, eyes, legs.
1. queen   2. strong
3. antennae   4. 6

p. 56:

2. 2 + 6 = 8, 6 + 2 = 8
3. 3 + 7 = 10, 7 + 3 = 10
4. 1 + 8 = 9, 8 + 1 = 9.
7, 8, 6, 4, 1, 5, 3, 2.

p. 57:

1. A man had a bag of sand.
2. I can swim all day.
3. The mouse ate the cheese.
4. exclamation marks circled.

p. 58:

1. inches   2. gallons 3. pounds
4. ounces 5. pounds 6. inches
7. ounces 8. inches 9. pounds.

p. 59:

strong/weak, fast/slow, over/under, in/out, clean/dirty, tall/short.
1. open   2. messy   3. truth
4. always   5. stop.

p. 60:

1. <,	2. >,	3. =
4. >,	5. <,	6. <,
7. =	8. >	9. =
10. 17	11. 12	12. 16
13. 21	14. 23	15. 21

80, 100, 120, 140, 60, 180, 200, 220.

p. 61:

oa, ee, oa, ee, oa, oa, ee, oa, oa, ee.
1. some   2. went   3. know
4. about   5. house.

p. 62:

1. 1/2 circle colored,2
2. 1/3 square colored,3
3. 1/4 rectangle colored,4
4. 1/2
5. 1/3
6. 1/4
7. 1/4

p. 63:

Answers vary.

p. 67:

1. solid   2. liquid   3. gas
4. space   5. solid, liquid, gas.
6. S,G,S,L,L,G.

p. 68:

1. 8 + 2 =102. 5 – 3 =2
3. 6 + 5 =11.

p. 69:

1. hello   2. Nice
3. sorry   4. open
5. thank you
6. excuse me
7. please   8. May
    please, excuse me, thank you, may I.

p. 70:

1. .45   2. .75
3. .30   4. .80
5. .60 cents – .30 cents
    = .30 cents.
6. .40 cents + .40 cents
    = .80 cents.

p. 71:

circled items: shoe, house, watermelon, tomato, soap, carrot, clothes. Answers vary

p. 72:

1. 2,2,8,8,4,8,15,10,14.
2. 49,13,20,7,25,36,75,9.
3. 13,23,30,35,61,113,101,106.
4. 30,50,20,40,80,60,100,90.

p. 73:

1. duck   2. ram   3. cupcake
4. skis   5. spider   6. frog
7. top   8. hand   9. pig.

p. 74:

1. 2 ,2   2. 3,4   3. 5,9
4. 1,9   5. 8,5   6. 7,0
7. 12,16,19. 8. 13,23,33 9.
    43,47,49.
10. 16,60,96
11. 4,8,12,16,20, 24,28.

Use a timer to motivate your child to stay on task and finish their work in a timely manner.

Answer Key

p. 75:
seat, black, courage, herself and others.

p. 79:
mister=Mr. inch=in. street=st. feet= ft. January=Jan. Sunday=Sun. Wednesday=Wed. August=Aug. October=Oct. Friday=Fri. February=Feb. Saturday= Sat. Tuesday =Tues. September=Sept. November =Nov.

p. 80:
1. 5 + 4 = 9, 4 + 5 = 9
2. 7 + 3 = 10, 3 + 7 = 10
3. 5, 8 – 3 = 5
4. 12 – 8 = 4
5. 12 – 4 = 8
6. 9 – 3 = 6
7. 9 – 6 = 3.

p. 81:
1. mail carrier
2. doctor
3. grocer
4. teacher
5. dentist
6. police officer
7. firefighter

p. 82:
1. 14   2. 10   3. 8
4. 15   5. 7   6. 5
7. 12   8. 11   9. 3
10. 0
11. hands drawn.
12. 6,12,18,24,30.

p. 83:
sh,ch,ch,sh,sh,sh,ch,sh.
1. We are going to the beach.
2. The ball is in the tree.
3. Is the ship sailing across the sea?
4. Can you climb the peach tree?

p. 84:
1. East   2. the
   pond
3. the bench   4. Franklin Park
5. north   6. cart circled

p. 85:
1. Pacific Ocean
2. Indian Ocean
3. Atlantic Ocean
4. Arctic Ocean
5. Southern Ocean
6. North America
7. Asia
8. Australia
9. Africa
10. Europe

p. 86:
1. triangle, 3,3
2. rectangle, 4,4
3. pentagon, 5,5.
4. octagon, 8,8.
5. 3 more triangles to make a rectangle.
6. a circle.

p. 87:
India, war, hurt, respect.

p. 91:
bee   2. two   3. sun
4. knight   5. bear   6. pair
7. nose   8. meet   9. sea
10. four.

p. 92:
1. 32   2. 56   3. 44
4. 16   5. 86   6. 36
7. 78   8. 1
9. 8, 12, 6, 10, 22, 4, 16.
10. 3, 5, 13, 7, 11, 15, 77.

p. 93:
Answers vary.

p. 94:
Answers vary.

p. 95:
1. She   2. They   3. We
4. It   5. We, them
6. her   7. them

p. 96:
1. 12/2, 15/5, 16/6, 18/8, 19/9, 17/7, 14/4, 13/3.
2. 2nd bank circled.

p. 97:
circled foods: pretzel, apple, cheese, milk, bread, corn, banana, carrot.
Crossed out: cookie, soda, candy, chips. Picture varies.

p. 98:
1. cube,no,yes.
2. pyramid,no,no.
3. cylinder, yes,yes.
4. sphere, yes,no.
5. pentagon
6. hexagon
7. answers vary.

Have your child correct their own work while you read off the answers. This will reinforce the skills they just practiced.

1-2 • © Summer Fit Activities™

Answer Key

p. 99:

Remember to take my lunch; Admit what I did; Wear my helmet; Clean my room.

p. 103:

circled items: penny, flute, paperclip, fork, key, dime, nail, nickel.

p. 104:

1. 60 minutes
2. 3 feet
3. 60 seconds
4. 12 months
5. 16 ounces
6. 11   7. 11   8. 14
9. $1.62   10. $2.39

p. 105:

1. shadow
2. bigger
3. greedy
4. Be content with what you have, don't be greedy.

p. 106:

1. 5, 6, 7, 8, 9, 10
2. purple number: 10, 18, 42, 20. Yellow numbers: 11, 15, 35.

p. 107:

1. 1,5,4,2,3.   2. 4,5,3,2,1.

p. 108:

1. Maddie, Tyler, Carlos, Gabe, Sam, Joe.
2. Grace, Noah, Sophie, Max, Pedro.
3. David, Lucy.

p. 109:

mammals:
    tiger, monkey, dog.
Birds:
    eagle, robin, owl.
Reptiles:
    lizard, snake, turtle.
Insects:
    grasshopper, fly, ladybug.

p. 110:

1. 1 hundreds, 4 tens, 6 ones, 146.
2. 3 hundreds, 8 tens, 9 ones, 389. 6, 7, 8, 0, 3, 2, 5, 9; 5, 2, 1, 3, 8, 3, 9, 4.

p. 111:

shark, arm, fear, surf, dreams.

p. 115:

oa, ou, oa, oa, ou, oa, ou, oa, oa

p. 116:

1. apple   2. pretzel   3. candy
4. car   5. nickel   6. .65

p. 117:

1. pail   2. sunglasses
3. ball   4. umbrella
5. waves   6. sand castle
7. starfish   8. shovel.

p. 118:

1. 1/4   2. 1/6   3. 1/2
4. 20, 30   5. 10, 20   6. 75, 85
7. 125, 135 8. 40, 60   9. 65, 85
10. 135, 155 11. 80, 100
12. 80, 108, 118, 180, 188.

p. 119:

1. brown
2. plants, bark from trees.
3. dam   4. paddle
5. streams 6. lodge.

p. 120:

2. 8   3. 300   4. 50
5. 100   6. 40   7. 3
8. 100   9. 143   10. 526
11. 852   12. 258

p. 121:

Answers vary.

p. 122:

1. 60   2. 12   3. 24
4. 12   5. 60   6. 12
7. 99   8. 99   9. 98
10. 128   11. 3   12. Tuesday
13. 552   14. 276   15. 365

p. 123:

Check drawn lines. No line to Animal Ambulance.

Give your student an opportunity to rework missed questions. Go over any mistakes made together.

Summer Fit Book Report I

Title:

_____

- -

_____

Author:

_____

- -

_____

Illustrator:

_____

- -

_____

Setting (Where the story takes place):

_____

- -

_____

Main Character(s):

_____

- -

_____

Write your favorite part of the story (use separate sheet of paper if needed):

_____

- -

_____

_____

- -

_____

Tell your favorite part of the story to a parent, guardian or friend.

Read a variety of books on topics that interest you already and new areas that you want to explore!

Summer Fit Book Report II

Title:

Author:

Illustrator:

Setting (Where the story takes place):

Main Character(s):

Write your favorite part of the story (use separate sheet of paper if needed):

Tell your favorite part of the story to a parent, guardian or friend.

Read a variety of books on topics that interest you already and new areas that you want to explore!

Summer Fit Book Report III

Title:

Author:

Illustrator:

Setting (Where the story takes place):

Main Character(s):

Write your favorite part of the story (use separate sheet of paper if needed):

Tell your favorite part of the story to a parent, guardian or friend.

> Read a variety of books on topics that interest you already and new areas that you want to explore!

Summer Fit Book Report IV

Title:

_____

- -

Author:

_____

- -

Illustrator:

_____

- -

Setting (Where the story takes place):

_____

- -

Main Character(s):

_____

- -

Write your favorite part of the story (use separate sheet of paper if needed):

_____

- -

_____

- -

_____

Tell your favorite part of the story to a parent, guardian or friend.

Read a variety of books on topics that interest you already and new areas that you want to explore!

HEALTH
&
NUTRITION

Summer Fit Activities
Published by Active Planet Kids

Let's Play

There are so many ways to play! Check off the different activities as you play them, have fun!

Everybody has different abilities and interests, so take the time to figure out what activities and exercises you like. Try them all: soccer, dance, karate, basketball and skating are only a few. After you have played a lot of different ones, go back and focus on the ones you like! Create your own ways to be active and combine different activities and sports to put your own twist on things. Talk with your parents or caregiver for ideas and have them help you find and do the activities that you like best. Playing and exercising is a great way to help you become fit, but remember that the most important thing about playing is that you are having fun!

List of Exercise Activities

Home–Outdoor:

Walking
Ride Bicycle
Swimming
Walk Dog
Golf with whiffle balls outside
Neighborhood walks/Exploring
(in a safe area)
Hula Hooping
Rollerskating/Rollerblading
Skateboarding
Jump rope
Climbing trees
Play in the back yard
Hopscotch
Stretching
Basketball
Yard work
Housecleaning

Home – Indoor:

Dancing
Exercise DVD
Yoga DVD
Home gym equipment
Stretch bands
Free weights
Stretching

With friends or family:

Red Rover
Chinese jump rope
Regular jump rope
Ring around the rosie
Tag/Freeze
Four score
Capture the flag
Dodgeball
Slip n Slide
Wallball
Tug of War
Stretching
Run through a sprinkler
Skipping
Family swim time
Bowling
Basketball
Hiking
Red light, Green light
Kick ball
Four Square
Tennis
Frisbee
Soccer
Jump Rope
Baseball

Turn off TV Go Outside - PLAY!
Public Service Announcement
Brought to you by Summer Fit

Chill out on Screen Time

Screen time is the amount of time spent watching TV, DVDs or going to the movies, playing video games, texting on the phone and using the computer. The more time you spend looking at a screen the less time you are outside riding your bike, walking, swimming or playing soccer with your friends. Try to spend no more than a couple hours a day in front of a screen for activities other than homework and get outside and play!

1-2 • © Summer Fit Activities™

HEALTHY BODIES

There are many ways to enrich your life by eating healthy, exercising each day and playing! Keeping your body strong and healthy will help you feel good and even perform better in school. To be healthy, you need to eat right, get enough sleep and exercise. What you learn and do with Summer Fit Activities™ is just the beginning. From here, you will be able to find other healthy and active things to do based on your interests, abilities and personal goals.

 Aerobic Exercises help your cardiovascular system that includes your heart and blood vessels. You need a strong heart to pump blood. Your blood delivers oxygen and nutrients to your body.

 Strength Exercises help you make your muscles stronger and increase your muscular endurance. Endurance helps you get the most from your muscles before you get tired!!

 Flexibility Exercises are good for many reasons including warming up before you do aerobic or strength exercises. Flexibility also helps you use all your muscles in different ways, positions and ranges of motion.

Your body composition is made up of lean mass and fat mass. Lean mass includes water, muscles and organs in your body. Fat mass includes fat your body needs for later and stores for energy.

Exercise helps you burn body fat and do more of the activities you want to do like hiking, biking and playing at the beach. There are a lot fun sports and activities to choose from that will help you strengthen your body and your brain!

Get Active!

Apple	Brain
Water	Vegetable
Exercise	Muscles
Aerobic	Organs
Strength	Fun
Flexibility	Play

```
D G L H B J S Z V Z B R F P C
Y H V T T E V E V A Z Y L F I
A C U P L G G M Y K I V E S B
G O T C A E N G H T P W X M O
H E S X T L M E Y A L P I L R
A U Y A E S I C R E X E B V E
M P B Y B M R G B T H Z I Q A
I L P R O L S V V F S R L K X
E Y A L D P E N B G A R I I I
F I B P E L H Y U V I F T W N
N G T D J A U D L F Z Q Y A X
O N M C X A V R S I V J S T J
O R G A N S B W A K K R A E C
J T C E L Y R C U Z R B G R P
X J P Y A W W E O S C K I K J
```

Active Lifestyle Pop Quiz!

What does being active mean to <u>you</u>?

List your 3 favorite aerobic activities

1) _____

2) _____

3) _____

EX:
bicycling, running, swimming, skateboarding, hiking

List 2 sports you like to play

1) _____

2) _____

EX:
lacrosse, basketball, baseball, dance, volleyball

List 3 activities you like that help build strength and flexibility

1) _____

2) _____

3) _____

EX:
yoga, dance, gymnastics, martial arts, jump rope

List 3 fun things you like to do that get you moving

1) _____

2) _____

3) _____

EX:
bowling, skating, fishing, gardening, cooking

List 2 things you can limit that will help you be more active:

1) _____

2) _____

EX:
video games, TV, phone

List 3 things you can do to help the environment and get you moving more often!

1) _____

2) _____

3) _____

EX:
pick up trash in neighborhood, separate items in recycling bins, help plant a garden, wash your water cup and reuse, ride your bike

1-2 • © Summer Fit Activities™

Summer Fitness Program

The goal of your Summer Fitness program is to help you improve in all areas of physical fitness and to be active every day.

You build cardiovascular endurance through aerobic exercise. For aerobic exercise, you need to work large muscle groups that get your heart pumping and oxygen moving through your entire body. This increases your heart rate and breathing. On your aerobic day, you can jog, swim, hike, dance, skateboard, ride your bike, roller blade... there are so many to choose from

Your goal should be to try to get 30 minutes a day of aerobic exercise at least 2-3 times a week. Follow your daily Summer Fit™ exercise schedule and choose your own aerobic exercises along the way.

You build your muscular strength and muscle endurance with exercises that work your muscles, like push-ups, sit-ups and pull-ups. Increase how many you can do of each of these over time and pay attention to your Summer Fit ™daily exercises for other activities that help build strong muscles.

Get loose – stretch. Warming up before you exercise if very important. It prepares your body for exercising by loosening your muscles and getting your body ready for training. An easy start is to shake your arms and roll your shoulders!

Time to Hydrate

It is important to drink water before and after you exercise because water regulates your body temperature and gives you nutrients to keep you healthy.

The next time you exercise, drink a cup of water before and after you are done.

Color the bottom half of the cup red below to represent the water you drink before you exercise. Color the top half of the cup blue to represent the water you drink after you exercise.

Water Facts

There is the same amount of water on earth today as there was when dinosaurs roamed through our backyards!

75% of your brain is water!

Water regulates the earth's temperature.

Water is made up of two elements, hydrogen and oxygen. Its chemical formula is H2O

Water is essential for life on earth.

1-2 • © Summer Fit Activities™

Here are instructions for your daily exercises. Talk with a parent about setting goals. Set your goals for time or reps. Keep track of your goals using your Summer Fitness Chart. Have fun!

Aerobic Exercises and Activities

Tag: Decide who is "IT." Choose the boundaries for the game. If a player crosses the boundaries, during the game he/she is automatically "IT."

Give players a 15 second head start. "IT" counts to 15 and then chases the others to tag them! The player who has been tagged is now "IT!"

Foot Bag: Everybody who wants to play gathers in a circle about four or five feet across. Serve the foot bag by tossing it gently, about waist high. Keep the foot bag in the air using any part of your body except arms or hands. Pass the foot bag back and forth around the circle as long as possible without it touching the ground.

Tree Sprints: Use two trees that are 10-15 feet apart. Start with your left leg touching the base of the tree. On "Go" sprint as fast as you can to the opposite tree, touch the tree trunk, and sprint back to your start position. Continue sprints until you complete your goal or get tired.

Jumping Jacks: Stand with your back straight and knees crouched down a little. Place your arms at your side. Jump in place, raising your hands above your head and clapping while moving your feet apart. Count each time you clap your hands. Continue until you reach your goal or get tired.

Cross-Country Skier: Start in a medium crouch position with one leg in front of the other. Lean forward slightly, keep your knees flexed and bounce in place switching your front foot with your rear foot while swinging your arms back and forth with each bounce. Count 1 rep for each time you reach your start position. Continue until you reach your goal or get tired.

Hide and Seek: Select an area to play. Designate a specific area with clear boundaries. Have everyone gather around a tree or other landmark, which is "home base." Whoever goes first must close his/her eyes and count to 10. Everybody else hides during the count. After the count is over, call out "Ready or not here I come!" Now it's time to look for the other players who are hiding. They are trying to get to home base before they are found. If they get to home base without being found they are "safe." The first player found loses and they start the next game by counting to 10!

Turtle and Rabbit: This is a running exercise that you do by running in place. Start in turtle mode by running 25 steps in place very slowly. Then, be a rabbit and run 25 steps as fast as you can!

Wheel Over: Lie down on your back. Raise your legs off the ground and pretend you are riding your bike in the air. Try to keep your back flat on the floor or ground.

Run or Jog: Jog or run in your backyard or neighborhood. Pump your arms, keep your back straight, flex your knees, and stay on your toes. Continue for as long as you can or until you reach your time goal.

Toss and Run (bean bag): Find a start place in your backyard or neighborhood park. Toss your beanbag in front of you 5 feet. Walk to pick it up. Toss your beanbag 10 feet. Jog to pick it up. Toss your beanbag 15 feet. Run as fast as you can to pick it up! Repeat as many times as needed to complete your goal. If space is limited, toss back and forth to the same place.

Freeze Tag: In Freeze Tag, everybody tries to stay away from whomever is "It." When you are tagged, you "freeze" in your tracks until somebody unfreezes you by crawling between your legs without being tagged themselves. When somebody is tagged for the third time, he/she is "It!"

Egg Race (spoon and egg): Mark a start and finish line 10-15 feet away. Balance an egg on a spoon and race to the finish line! Whomever crosses first wins, but be careful, if you drop your egg you lose!

Scissor Swim: Lie down on your stomach. Raise your legs 6-8 inches up and down like scissors. Pretend you are cutting the water like a huge pair of scissors! Keep your legs straight and your stomach flat on the ground.

Stepping on Up: Climb the stairs in your house or apartment. Raise your legs high on each step. Climb slow and steady. Set a goal on how many steps you can climb.

Hill Run (Jog): Find a hill at a park or neighborhood. Run (or jog) up the hill. Pump your arms, keep your back straight, flex your knees, and stay on your toes. Set a goal on how many times you can run (or jog) the hill.

Hi Yah!: Stand with both your feet planted on the ground. When you are ready, kick the air with one leg and scream, "Hi-Yah!" When your foot is planted, kick your other leg, "Hi-Yah!" Go slow and set a goal on how many times you can kick without losing your balance.

Wild: Find an area in your backyard or park. Run, scream, wave your hands in the air, jump up and down, roll on the grass – have fun!

Strength Exercises and Activities

Ankle Touches: Lie with your back on the ground. Bend your knees up with your feet flat on the ground. Alternate from left to right touching left hand to left heel and right hand to right heel.

Push-ups: Lie chest-down with your hands at shoulder level, palms flat on the floor, and feet together. Let yourself down slowly as far as you can go. Straighten your arms and push your body up off the floor. Try not to bend as you push up. Pause for a moment before you do another. Set a goal on how many you can do in a row.

Moon Touches: Stand with both feet together and back straight. Bend your knees and both arms in front of your body. Jump straight up with both feet and reach up as you jump with your left and then your right arm. Set a goal on how many you can do without stopping.

Sky Reach: Choose a small object such as a ball, a book or even a piece of fruit. Make an "L" with your arm—with your upper arm at shoulder level and your forearm pointing toward the ceiling. Now extend your arm straight over your shoulder, pushing the object toward the sky. Return to your starting position.

Fly in the Ointment: Stand straight with your arms stretched out and opened wide. Keep your back straight and bend your knees just a little bit. Slowly touch one knee to the floor while clapping your hands. Return to starting position and start over by touching the opposite knee to the floor and clapping.

Jump Rope: Start by holding an end of the rope in each hand. Position the rope behind you on the ground. Raise your arms up and turn the rope over your head bringing it down in front of you. When it reaches the ground, jump over it. Find a good pace, not too slow and not too fast. Jump over the rope each time it comes around. Continue until you reach your goal of jumping a certain amount of times without stopping.

Bear Crawl: Crouch down on your hands and feet. Slowly move forward stretching your arms out as far as you can in front of you. Stay low on all fours and growl like a bear! How many times can you go around your yard on all fours?

Hula-Hoop: Hold the hula-hoop around your waist with both hands. Pull it forward so it is resting against your back. With both hands, fling the hoop to the left so that rolls in a circle around your body. Do this a few times until you get the feel of it. Leave the hula-hoop on the ground for a few minutes and practice swirling your hip. Move your pelvis left, back, right, forward. Find a groove and keep the hoop going around your hips as long as you can. When it falls to the ground pick it up and try again!

Crab Crawl: Sit on the ground with your arms behind you and your legs in front. Move your legs forward followed by your arms. Watch out for sand traps!

Modified Push Up: Get in your push-up position and then rest on your knees on the ground. When you are ready to start, lower your body straight down while rocking forward on your knees to help take away some of your body weight. Push back up so you are in your original position. This is a great way to start learning push-ups and building your strength.

Freeze Dance: Play this with your friends! Put on your favorite music and dance! When the music stops, everybody freezes!

Bottle curls: Start with two bottles of laundry detergent (or any large bottle with a handle). Stand with your feet flat on the floor, shoulder width apart. Place both your hands in the same position on the handles of each bottle. With your back straight, slowly curl each bottle keeping your arm in the shape of an "L" until the bottle is raised to your shoulder. Only use bottles that you can lift easily and that do not cause you to stumble under their weight.

Snake Curl: Lie on your back with knees bent, feet flat on the ground, and a beanbag between your knees to keep them together. Lay your hands on your side. Curl up and lay back in your starting position. Repeat!

Chair Leg-lifts: Put a small chair next to you. Standing next to the chair, rest one hand lightly on the back (the back of the chair is facing you). Slowly lift one leg with your knee bent. Now, slowly lower your leg until your foot almost touches the ground. How many can you do?

Giraffe Walk: Stand up tall with your feet firmly planted on the floor. Keep your back straight and upright. Reach your arms over your head and skip forward twice. Then, slowly walk forward twice again and do another skip.

Can Do: Go to the kitchen and find two of the heaviest cans you can hold. Stand with your feet flat on the floor, with the cans in your hands and arms at your side. Lift the cans up to your chest, bending your arms at the elbows. Hold for two seconds, and then slowly lower your arms.

Bottle Lift: Start with two bottles of laundry detergent (or any large bottle with a handle). Stand with your feet flat on the floor, shoulder width apart. Place the bottles on each side of your feet. Bend your knees, grab the bottles and stand up.

Bunny Bounce: Stand with feet together, knees slightly bent and hands touching your ears. Hop first on your right foot and then on your left. Now, jump with both feet spread apart and then continue hopping, first on the right, then on the left foot!

Crab Kick: Get down in a crab position with your body supported with your hands and feet, and your back towards the ground. Keep your seat up and let your body sag. Kick your right leg in the air. After you have done this 5-10 times switch to your left and repeat.

Gorilla Walk: Spread your feet apart as wide as your shoulders. Bend at your waist and grab your ankles. Hold your ankles and walk stiff legged.

Milk Bottle Lifts: Clean and rinse out 2 quart plastic milk bottles. Fill them with water and screw the caps on tight. Slowly lift them up over your head by extending your arm straight up. Once you do the right, return to starting position. Extend your left arm and repeat. Alternate between arms.

1-2 • © Summer Fit Activities™

NUTRITION

Hey Parents!

A healthy diet and daily exercise will maximize the likelihood of your child growing up healthy and strong. Children are constantly growing and adding bone and muscle mass, so a balanced diet is very important to their overall health. Try to provide three nutritious meals a day that all include fruits and vegetables. Try to limit fast food and cook at home as often as you can. Not only is it better on your pocketbook, cooking at home is better for you and can be done together as a family. Everyone can help and it is more likely you will eat together as a family.

As a healthy eating goal, avoid food and drinks that are high in sugar as much as possible. Provide fresh fruits, vegetables, grains, lean meats, chicken, fish and low-fat dairy items as much as possible.

5 Steps to Improve Eating Habits

 Make fresh fruits and vegetables readily available

 Cook more at home, and sit down for dinner as a family.

 Limit sugary drinks, cereals and desserts

 Serve smaller portions

 Limit snacks to 1 or 2 daily

HEALTHY EATING POP QUIZ!

What does eating
healthy mean to <u>you</u>?

List your 3 favorite healthy foods:

1) _____   2) _____   3) _____

If you were only to eat vegetables,
what 5 vegetables would you choose?

1) _____   2) _____

3) _____   4) _____   5) _____

Fill in the names of 5 different food groups on the Food Plate.

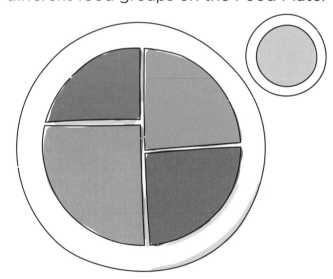

Circle the food and drink items that are healthy foods from the list below:

Milk	Apple	Chicken	Salad
candy	butter	soda	orange
ice cream	carrot	cotton candy	chocolate shake

List your 3 favorite healthy foods

1) _____   2) _____   3) _____

Create a list of foods you would like to grow in a garden

Nutrition – *Food Plate*

It is important to eat different foods from the 5 different food groups. Eating a variety of foods helps you stay healthy. Some foods give you protein and fats. Other foods give you vitamins, minerals and carbohydrates. Your body needs all of these to grow healthy and strong!

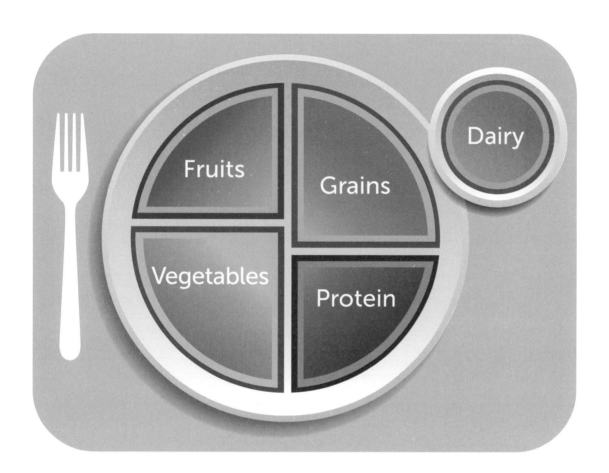

List 3 different foods for each category.

Fruits	Vegetables	Grains	Protein	Dairy
1) _____	1) _____	1) _____	1) _____	1) _____
2) _____	2) _____	2) _____	2) _____	2) _____
3) _____	3) _____	3) _____	3) _____	3) _____

Nutrition – *Meal Planner*

Plan out 3 balanced meals for one day.
Organize your meals so you will eat all the
recommended foods listed on the Food Plate.

BREAKFAST

LUNCH

DINNER

Nutrition – *Meal Tracker*

Use these charts to list the different foods from the different food categories on My Plate that you eat each day.
Every day you mark each food category color in the vegetable!

	Grains	Dairy	Protein	Fruits	Vegetables	
Monday						
Tuesday						
Wednesday						
Thursday						
Friday						
Saturday						
Sunday						

	Grains	Dairy	Protein	Fruits	Vegetables	
Monday						
Tuesday						
Wednesday						
Thursday						
Friday						
Saturday						
Sunday						

MY OWN HEALTHY SNACKS

Frozen Banana Slices

Prep Time: 10 minutes

Freezer Time: 2 hours

Yield: 2 servings, Good for all ages!

Ingredients: 2 fresh bananas

Directions: Peel the bananas and cut them into 5-6 slices each. Place the banana slices on a plate and place in freezer for 2 hours. Enjoy your frozen banana snack on a hot summer day!

Yogurt Parfaits

Prep Time: 15 minutes

Cook Time: 0 minutes

Yield: 4 servings, Good for all ages!

Ingredients: 2 cups fresh fruit, at least 2 different kinds (can also be thawed fresh fruit)
1 cup low-fat plain or soy yogurt
4 TBSP 100% fruit spread
1 cup granola or dry cereal

Directions: Wash and cut fruit into small pieces. In a bowl, mix the yogurt and fruit spread together. Layer each of the four parfaits as follows: Fruit Yogurt Granola (repeat) Enjoy!

Frozen Grapes

Prep Time: 10 minutes

Freezer Time: 2 hours

Yield: 4 servings, Good for all ages!

Ingredients: Seedless grapes

Directions: Wash seedless grapes and separate them from their stem. Place into a bowl or plastic bag. Put them into the freezer for 2 hours. Enjoy your cold, sweet and crunchy treat!

Fruit Smoothies

Prep Time: 5 minutes

Cook Time: 0 minutes

Yield: 2 servings, Good for all ages!

Ingredients: 1 cup berries, fresh or frozen
4 ounces Greek yogurt
1/2 cup 100% apple juice
1 banana, cut into chunks
4 ice cubes

Directions: Place apple juice, yogurt, berries and banana into blender. Cover and blend until smooth. While the blender is running, drop ice cubes into the blender one at a time. Blend until smooth. Pour and enjoy!

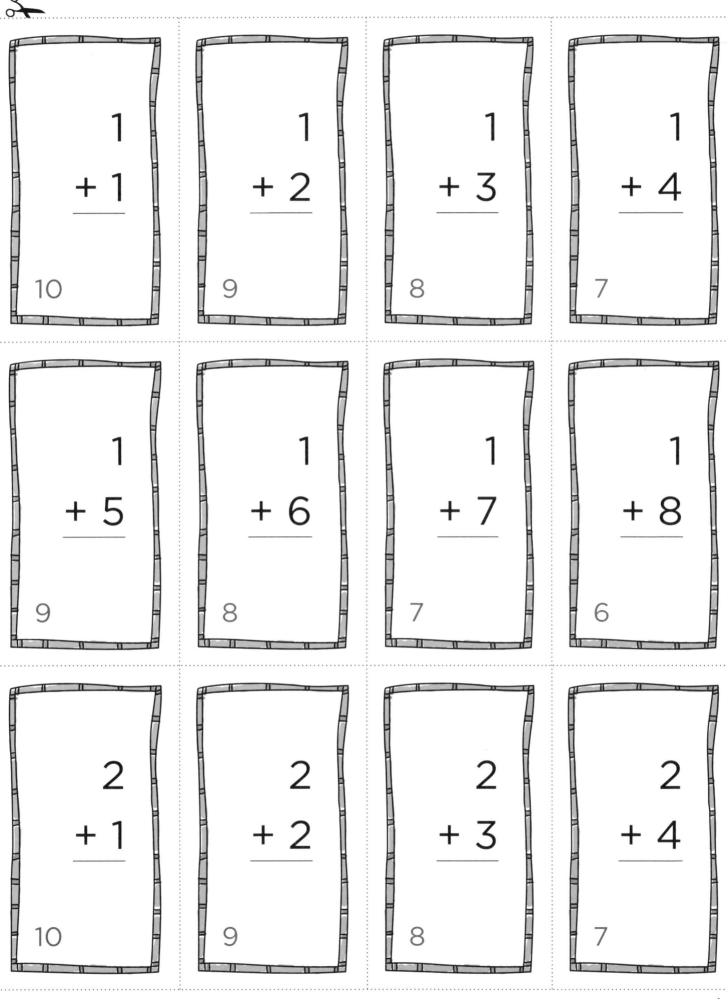

1
+ 1
_____
10

1
+ 2
_____
9

1
+ 3
_____
8

1
+ 4
_____
7

1
+ 5
_____
9

1
+ 6
_____
8

1
+ 7
_____
7

1
+ 8
_____
6

2
+ 1
_____
10

2
+ 2
_____
9

2
+ 3
_____
8

2
+ 4
_____
7

A

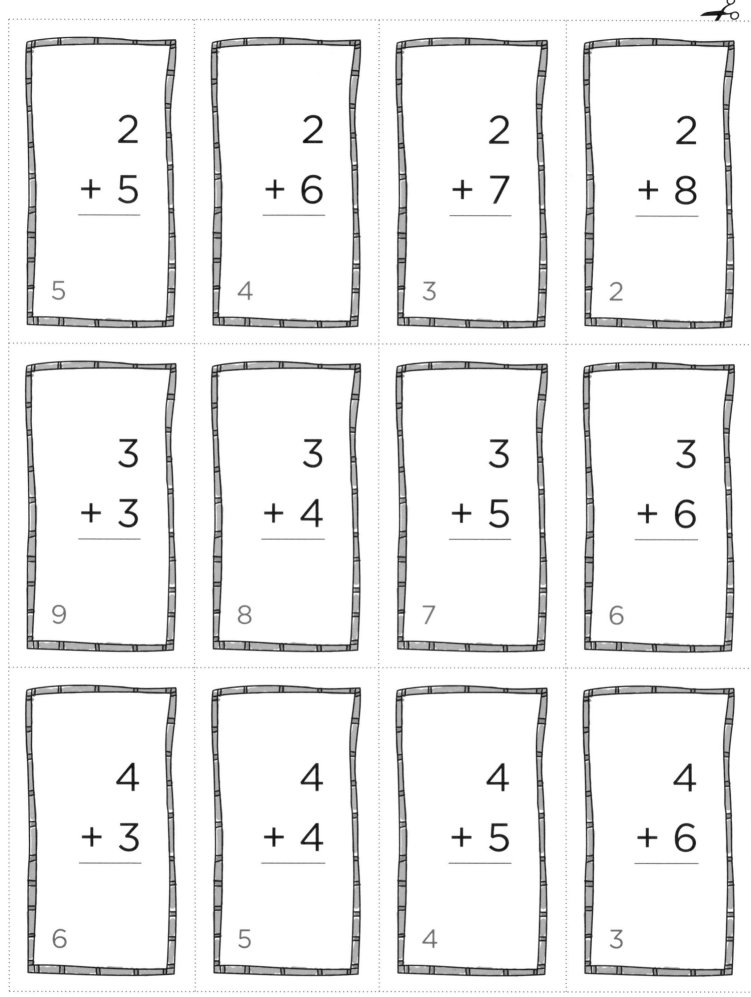

2
+ 5
———
5

2
+ 6
———
4

2
+ 7
———
3

2
+ 8
———
2

3
+ 3
———
9

3
+ 4
———
8

3
+ 5
———
7

3
+ 6
———
6

4
+ 3
———
6

4
+ 4
———
5

4
+ 5
———
4

4
+ 6
———
3

B

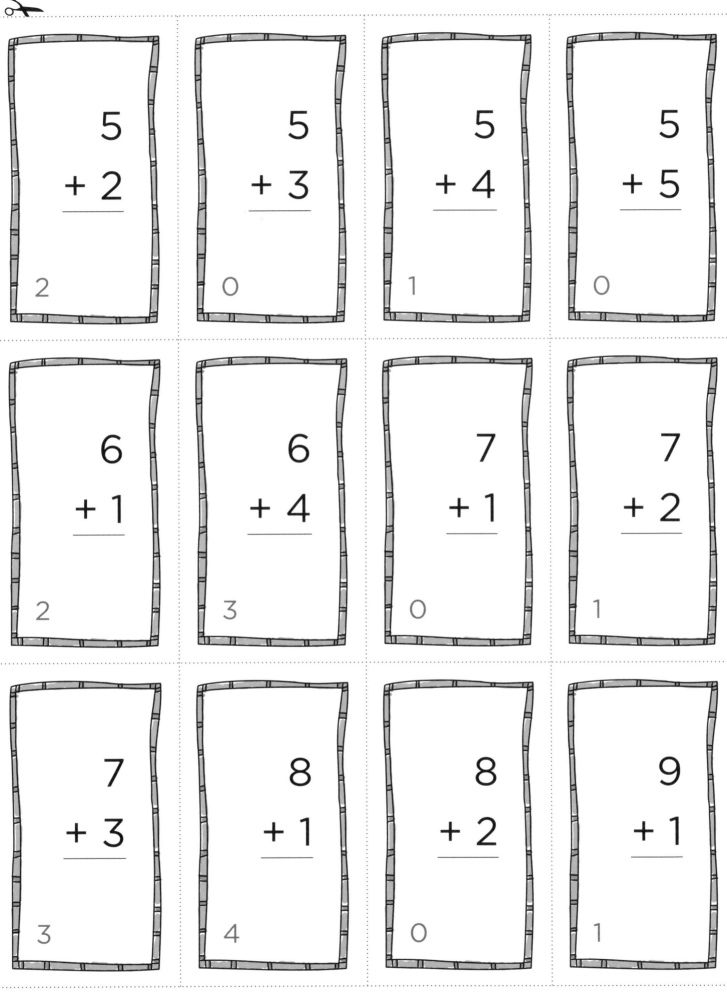

5
+ 2
___
2

5
+ 3
___
0

5
+ 4
___
1

5
+ 5
___
0

6
+ 1
___
2

6
+ 4
___
3

7
+ 1
___
0

7
+ 2
___
1

7
+ 3
___
3

8
+ 1
___
4

8
+ 2
___
0

9
+ 1
___
1

c

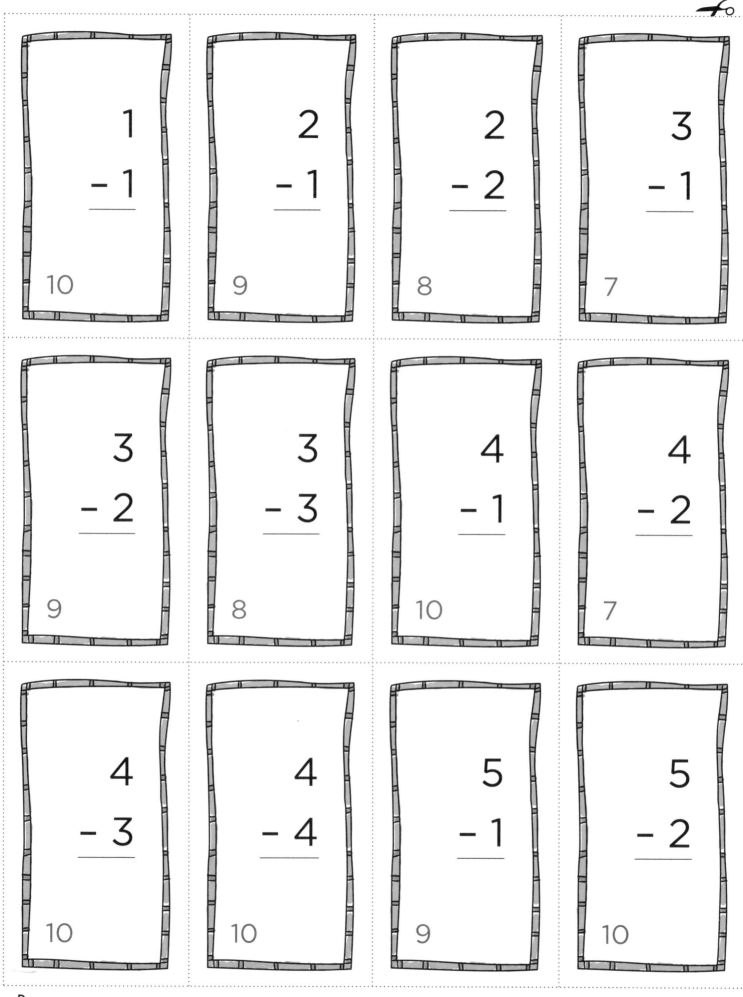

1
− 1
_____
10

2
− 1
_____
9

2
− 2
_____
8

3
− 1
_____
7

3
− 2
_____
9

3
− 3
_____
8

4
− 1
_____
10

4
− 2
_____
7

4
− 3
_____
10

4
− 4
_____
10

5
− 1
_____
9

5
− 2
_____
10

D

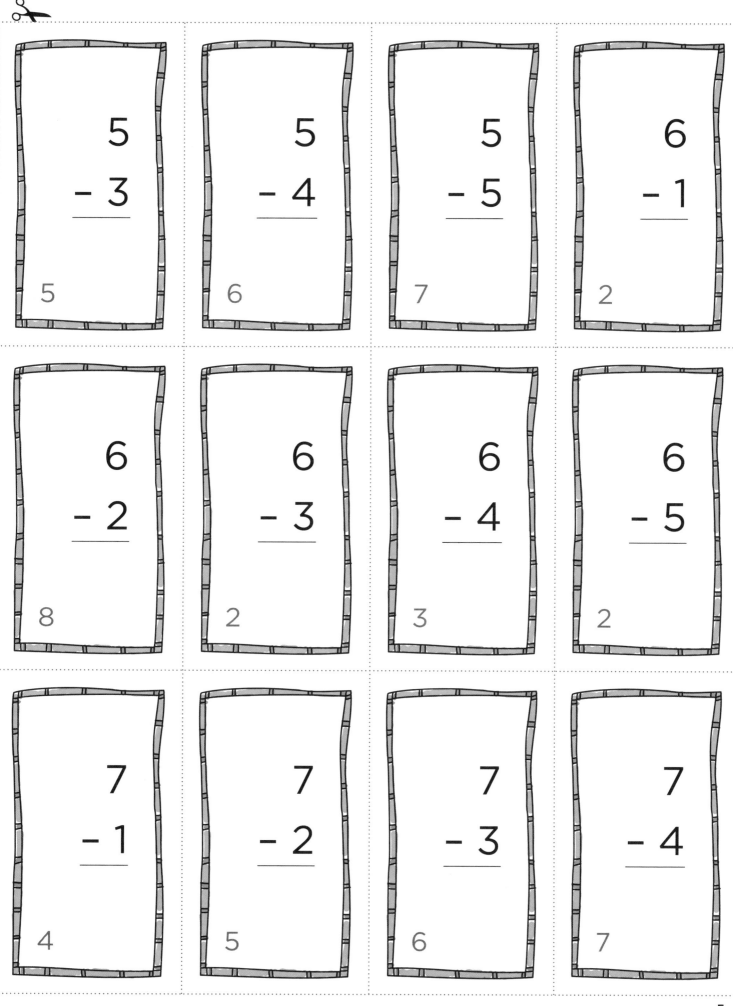

$$5 - 3$$
5

$$5 - 4$$
6

$$5 - 5$$
7

$$6 - 1$$
2

$$6 - 2$$
8

$$6 - 3$$
2

$$6 - 4$$
3

$$6 - 5$$
2

$$7 - 1$$
4

$$7 - 2$$
5

$$7 - 3$$
6

$$7 - 4$$
7

E

7 − 5 ___ 5	8 − 1 ___ 0	8 − 2 ___ 1	8 − 3 ___ 2
8 − 4 ___ 1	8 − 5 ___ 2	8 − 6 ___ 3	9 − 1 ___ 4
9 − 2 ___ 3	9 − 3 ___ 4	9 − 4 ___ 5	9 − 5 ___ 6

9
− 6
7

9
− 7
8

9
− 8
9

every

as

ask

by

could

after

again

an

any

G

hum

10
− 1

1

10
− 2

2

10
− 3

3

had

has

her

him

fly

from

give

giving

old

once

open

over

let

live

may

of

his

how

just

know

think	take	put
walk	thank	round
were	them	some
when	then	stop

Value of **Curiosity**

Value of **Humor**

Value of **Love**

Value of **Kindness**

Value of **Dedication**

Value of **Friendship**

Value of **Giving**

Value of **Saving**

Value of **Understanding**

Value of **Imagination**

Value of **Responsibility**

Value of **Helping**

Being friendly, generous, considerate

Deep affection and caring for another person

Positive state of mind, being funny

Desire to know or learn something

Preventing the waste of something

To offer or hand over something

Mutual trust and support between people

To be committed to a task or purpose

To contribute and offer assistance

Being accountable for your actions and other peoples

Ability to be creative and resourceful

Aware of, and interested in learning other people, ideas and beliefs

L

Value of
Truth

Value of
Belief

Value of
Respect

Value of
Courage

Value of
Honesty

Value of
Sharing

Value of
Patience

Value of
Determination

Value of
Caring

Value of
Foresight

Value of
Learning

Value of
Fantasy

A fact, belief or person that is accepted as being true

Trust, faith or confidence in someone or something

Admire someone for their abilities, qualities or achievements

Ability to do something that frightens you

Sincere, free of deceit

To give to others

Accept or tolerate without getting upset

Being resolute to an idea or purpose

Displaying kindness and concern for others

Being able to predict needs or what will happen in the future

Knowledge through experience, study or being taught

Being able to imagine the impossible

CERTIFICATE OF COMPLETION

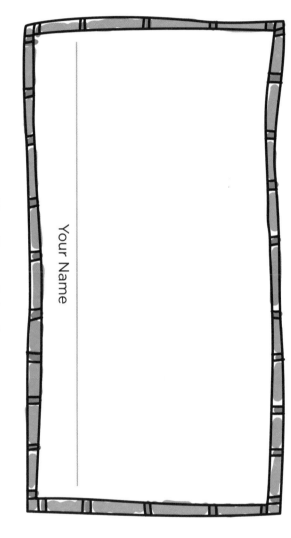

Has Completed

Your Name

Summer Fit Activities ™

Parent Signature

SummerFitActivities.com

Summer Fit Activities™

Published by Active Planet Kids